C000145216

Consequences

Diverse to Mosaic Britain?

Susan Popoola

Filament
Publishing

Published by Filament Publishing Ltd
16 Croydon Road, Waddon,
Croydon, Surrey, CRO 4PA UK
Telephone +44 (0)20 8688 2598
Fax +44 (0)20 7183 7186
info@filamentpublishing.com
www.filamentpublishing.com

Printed by Berforts Group - Stevenage and Hastings
Distributed by Gardners

ISBN 978-1-908691-08-8

Dedication

To my Mum, my Mother, and all those who have filled the gap and helped to shape me and enabled me to see beyond the surface into the various possibilities.

Acknowledgements

I would first and foremost like to acknowledge the British people in all their guises that make Britain such a fascinating place that inspired me to take the time to research and write this book.

The idea was undoubtedly mine, but I only started writing when a special friend of mine, Kriss Akabusi who encouraged me, held me to account, serving as an integral part of the journey until the job was done - thank you Kriss. I cannot, but also thank friends such as Heather Bradley who also supported me along the way in so many ways.

There are also those that shared their thoughts with me, questioned my thinking and took time to review earlier draft versions of the book such as Baroness Usha Prashar, David Pinchard, TopInterim, Jackie Adams-Bonitto, London Fire Brigade, Maureen Ghirelli, Organisation Development Consultant People, Solutions, Jane Gunn, Corporate Peacemakers and Rob Berkley, Director of Runnymede Trust.

Contents

21st Century Britain

Introduction - What's Going On!

We've got to find a way
To bring some lovin' ...
Marvin Gaye, What's Going On

The end of the first decade of the 21st century (2010) in Britain was sadly marked by students demonstrating over Government proposals and the eventual legislation on increased tuition fees. Whether you agree with tuition fees or not is one thing. But something that I believe is undeniable is the fact that the demonstrations were a reflection of the wider frustrations which started growing across the populace in 2008 and 2009; with the recession which has been made more painful to many, not so just because of the loss of work, but more so by the bonuses awarded to the employees within the banking sector that irked the public who had paid for the bail out of banks; the scandal over the inappropriate expenses of elected representatives i.e. MPs, followed up the austerity measures and the threat of loss of public sector jobs which while many see as crucial to economic recovery, others see as a threat to recovery from the recession. The feelings of shock and horror were possibly best portrayed on the face of the wife of Prince Charles, Camilla, when their car was unfortunately attacked during the student demonstrations in December 2010.

Sadly the discontent continued into 2011 with further demonstrations against the way in which spending cuts were being made, organised by the Trades Union Congress (TUC) in March 2011 and the largest public sector strike in five years in June 2011. Worst still were the August riots that started off in London which spread across different parts of the country. People questioned whether or not the riots were really about the shooting of a young black man by the police. That is open to debate. What is, however, unquestionable is that there are segments of society that are disengaged from the mainstream.

While some may believe that these are just passing incidents, there are many who look at the situation and are concerned that the levels of discontent are likely to be reflected across the country for years to come. The unfortunate thing is that for others discontent within this country is nothing new. They have been battling with it for years, if not decades. They feel undervalued, if not completely devalued, and question the future of the country and what it will be like in years to come for them and, most pertinently, for their children. It could be argued that they have a distorted understanding of the "what"s and the "why"s, but many people do not feel represented or listened to.

To be honest, I've always known this, but this was really and truly brought home to me during the summer of 2009. There were local elections that year and during the campaigning period I noticed that the British National Party (BNP) kept trending on Twitter[1]. Reading the tweets (i.e. Twitter messages) I realised that most of the people writing messages were not writing to declare their support for the BNP and to encourage people to vote. Rather, they were typically cursing and threatening people

---

[1]Just in case you don't know, Twitter is a social media tool which enables people to provide short updates on what's going on, what they're thinking about, etc.

who may have been considering voting for the BNP, calling them racist and stating in no uncertain terms what they believed should happen to them.

I must say, I in no way support the BNP and what they or other similar political parties and groups stand for, but the comments that I read did not sit well with me. This led me to think that there is a need to stop and try to understand what it is that would lead a mass of people to support the BNP, before we all start to sharpen our knives, as, though sometimes racism is very blatant and straightforward, I believe that at times it's actually difficult to determine what is racism or racist and what is people's ignorance and/or lack of understanding, or even mere desperation for help.

The questions in my mind were heightened when I happened to come across a list of local BNP members. Normally, I wouldn't have even looked at it, but because of the online communications that I had seen, I was curious. I was, however, surprised to see the name of a lady that I recently lunched with on the list. I was most especially surprised because she had actually asked me to work with her on a project. I was therefore left wondering was she a racist who simply thought that for whatever reason I was ok to work with? Alternatively, was she a person who had aligned herself to the BNP, not because she shared its root values, but because she believed it was the political party that came closest to representing her wider interests?

I haven't seen this particularly lady since the day that I had lunch with her, but the thoughts and questions in my mind have led me to the writing of this book. This book represents a journey to gain some understanding into what it is that leads everyday people to support the BNP, the National Front or other similar parties/groups, to understand how Britain has come to be such a diverse country and to look into how we ultimately need to live and work together.

My objective in writing this book is not to provide a complete historical account. Rather, my hope is to create a greater awareness and understanding of the issues in order to encourage people to look beyond the surface, openly discuss the issues and seek solutions.

A Bit of Context - British Demographics

Living life is fun and we've just begun
To get our share of the world's delights
High hopes we have for the future
And our goal's in sight...
Sister Sledge, We Are Family

Before I talk in more detail about groups such as the BNP and the typical issues and concerns that they and people who may feel inclined to support them have, I would like to set some further context by having a look at some of the characteristics that make up the British population.

The characteristics that I have focused on relate to ethnic origin/race; social economics; religion and age. Though I may later make mention of gender, sexual orientation and disability, I have not focused on them as I do not see them as the key areas of concern to this particular study.

I believe that the most precise information that is available comes from the 2001 population Census. This is, however, now 10 years old and therefore quite dated, as anyone who visited or lived in Britain in 2001 and has subsequently come back or lives here now, would know: within that timeframe the face of Britain has changed significantly. Over time, the way in which people identify themselves has also changed. For these reasons I've also looked at estimates and projections of demographics from sources such as the Office for National Statistics.

On Census Day 2001, Britain had a population of 58,789,194 - an increase of 1.5 million people (2.5%) from 1991. At the same time, 2007 projections for the 2008 population were 61.4 million, rising over 10 million to 71.6 by the year 2033. Of the additional 10 million, 7 million were projected to be based on migrants and additional population arising through the new migrants.

The ethnic breakdown was as follows:

Ethnic Group	Percentage
White British	85.67%
White Irish	1.20%
White (other)	5.27%
Indian	1.80%
Pakistani	1.60%
Bangladeshi	0.50%
Other Asian (non-Chinese)	0.40%
Black Caribbean	1.00%
Black African	0.80%
Black (other)	0.20%
Mixed race	1.20%
Chinese	0.40%
Other	0.40%

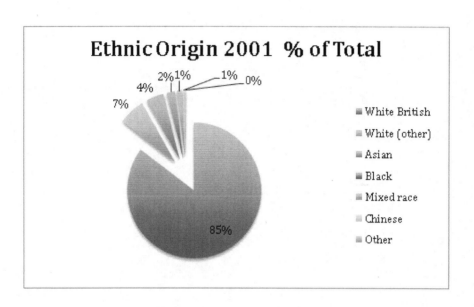

Ethnic Origin 2001 % of Total

- White British
- White (other)
- Asian
- Black
- Mixed race
- Chinese
- Other

Since 2001, the population was estimated to grow to over 54 million by the year 2007. In percentage terms, the White British of the population was predicted to change from 85% to 84%.

Ethnic Origin	Percentage
White British	84.26%
White Irish	1.08%
White (other)	3.39%
Indian	2.46%
Pakistani	1.70%
Bangladeshi	0.67%
Other Asian (non-Chinese)	0.64%
Black Caribbean	1.11%
Black African	1.36%
Black (other)	0.22%
Mixed race	1.65%
Chinese	0.76%
Other	0.71%

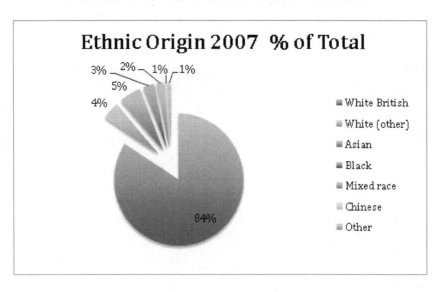

Ethnic Origin 2007 % of Total

3% 2% 1% 1%
5%
4%
84%

- White British
- White (other)
- Asian
- Black
- Mixed race
- Chinese
- Other

The 2001 Census showed **66%** of the population within the working age bracket of 15-64 years, with 18% under 15 and 16% in their retirement years.

Although the age bands were changed for the 2008 estimates, there is not much change in the groupings.

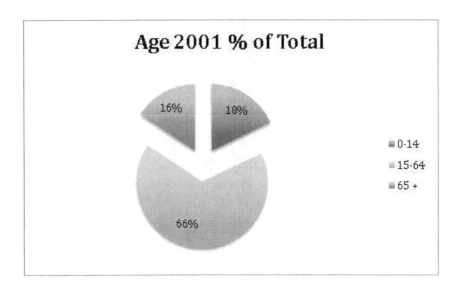

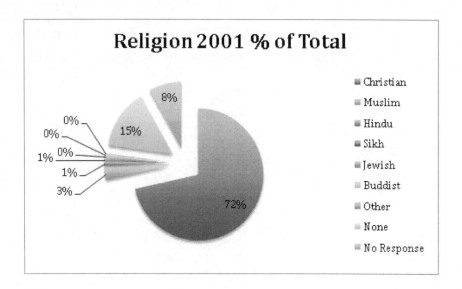

Religion 2001 % of Total

- Christian
- Muslim
- Hindu
- Sikh
- Jewish
- Buddist
- Other
- None
- No Response

72%
15%
8%
3%
1%
1%
0%
0%
0%

As of 2001, the Christian population constituted 71% of the total population. A key question if this percentage is reduced in future years is whether this is due to the growth of the proportion of other religions or due to a reduction in the proportion of the population that no longer sees itself as Christian.

These are just some basic statistics to provide a general overview. They don't, for instance, show the possible concentration of specific ethnic groups within an area or the age distribution of different ethnic groups. I don't want to bore people who aren't specifically interested in statistics to that level of detail. However, once we've reviewed the issues and concerns that people are raising, I will present some further statistics that may provide some context to these concerns and indicate whether the concerns are fact or fallacy.

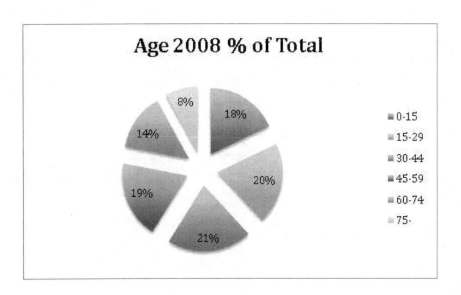

Age 2008 % of Total

- 0-15
- 15-29
- 30-44
- 45-59
- 60-74
- 75-

Nationalist Cry

Bring out the trumpets or perhaps a South African horn

BNP - Fringe Politics or Critical Viewpoints?

Send The Buggers Back
a BNP song
by Half a Shilling

If you lived in Britain and hadn't heard of the British National Party beforehand, you would have most definitely heard of it in September 2010 when there was a lot of controversy over the possible (and eventual) appearance of the party's Chairman, Nick Griffin, on the popular political programme Question Time.

But then again, just in case you were away, you don't watch Question Time, listen to news or don't interact with people who may have discussed this in any way, shape or form, I should explain.

The British National Party, commonly known as the BNP, is a British political party which emerged from the British National Front in 1982. As with the National Front, it is typical known as and referred to as right-wing, Fascist or even, at the extreme, Nazi. Its members, on the other hand, are more likely to describe the BNP simply as a nationalist party concerned about and fighting for the rights of indigenous British people who they see as becoming increasingly disadvantaged and marginalised in their own land.

I would venture to say that the BNP represents two groups of people which, through some of the subtleties of the messaging of the leadership and some core members, merge into each other.

There is the far-right, hateful element of the BNP with deep-rooted racists, nazistic tendencies that hates people whom they see as different, be they people of colour, Jews, homosexuals or what have you. These are the BNP members that will meet and burn effigies that represent black people, that have a deep-rooted and, dare I say, ungrounded hatred which would be very difficult if not out rightly futile to try and change. Furthermore, if you speak to the leadership of the BNP, the probability is that they will state that these people do not truly represent the views of the BNP even though, in many ways, the policies and positions held by the party fuel their point of view. Whatever the case, even though I have done some research on them, I really don't want to expend my energy or take up your time focusing on this group of people. There are a lot of grey areas between the two groups, but I believe that what is of most importance are the views of the second group of people who are aligned to the BNP out of love and concern for Britain and their personal interest.

In line with this, may I ask...have you seen the new BNP logo?

On the left, it has the Union flag on it in a heart shape with British National Party written to the right of it - a simple message I would venture to say: i.e. BNP members are people who love Britain. If the truth is to be told, even though the ideology and background basis may at times be a romanticised, narrow minded and distorted representation of reality, I don't for one minute question the love of the mainstream BNP members' love for Britain. I do however believe that there is also a lot of fear, confusion and misrepresentation of issues.

The Fear ... that Ultimately Leads to Confusion

Panic on the streets of London
Panic on the streets of Birmingham
I wonder to myself
Could life ever be sane again?
The Smiths, Panic

Right-wing politics is nothing new in Britain, it has been around for a long time - think of Oswald Mosley who formed the British Union of Fascists in 1932 with the aim of uniting the different fascist groups that were in existence. The British National Front itself dates back to 1967. I believe there is, however, a difference between it and the British National Party which, like no right-wing party before it, has attracted and gained the support of a much more mainstream audience - most especially under the leadership of Nick Griffin. As of the end of 2010, people have been rejoicing about reduced membership levels of the BNP. Even if it's remotely possible that the BNP may actually wither away in time, I believe it's premature to rejoice unless the issues that the party raises as concerns are addressed head-on. If the issues are not discussed in a way that the majority can understand, if the BNP disappeared it would simply be replaced by another or other groups such as the English Defence League which may actually be more right-wing than the BNP - I do believe that outside of core right-wing groups within the party, the BNP has actually toned down its message under Griffin.

But to the fear and confusion, I'd like to step back to 1968 which I believe was a critical year in British politics. It's before I was born, but one that stands out as it's the year in which Enoch Powell delivered his 'Rivers of Blood' speech in which he expressed grave concerns about Britain being overtaken by immigrants.

Powell said he was representing the views and concerns of his constituents. He'd also observed the race problems of America, the civil rights movement and the assassination of Martin Luther King Jr and feared similar racial problems in the UK.

It could be seen as an aside, but I don't believe that Powell simply represented the fears and views of the British people - he had a much broader knowledge and insight than they did. I don't mean to be rude, but I very much doubt that the typical working-class man in Britain had a clear knowledge of the civil rights movements in America and their impact even if they had heard that a man named Martin Luther King had been assassinated. I say this because I believe it's important as I don't believe that Powell simply represented the British people's point of view. Rather, he magnified a number of people's fears and birthed the fears of many others.

I think this is important because Powell was in a position of influence and therefore responsibility, which cannot be over-estimated. In as much as his fears were probably genuine, I would venture to say that his comparisons of the occurrences in America to what could potentially happen in Britain were overly simplified as he did not take cognisance of the variations in the history of the two countries. In America, large numbers of black people had lived in the country since 1619 as a result of slavery. Even when the slave trade came to an end, segregation and inequality remained. This was the root of the black American civil rights movement. Though there were questions around the equality and treatment of immigrants to Britain, the circumstances/ backdrop was entirely different and I will go ahead of myself and say that the question should have been on how immigration was better managed with proper integration and fairer treatment which the Equalities Act that Powell opposed was actually trying to propagate.

I think it's important for me to have stated this because I believe the reaction and fears that resulted from Powell's speech highlight the impact and importance of the words of people in authority be they people from the mainstream parties such as Powell or the right-wing parties such as the BNP itself, like John Tyndall who was Nick Griffin's very articulate predecessor.

If you know the history, you will be aware that following on from Powell's speech, he was sacked from the party the very next day. However a combination of the speech and his sacking led to widespread demonstrations amongst the British populace and I will say that the demonstrations were rooted in fear.

This is speculative, but I can't help but wonder whether people would have developed such deep-rooted fears if not for the speech of Enoch Powell. Sadly, I can't find any speeches that went out to directly address the fears that Powell's speech raised which means that the fears created or at best flamed were left to burn and be further flamed by the demonstrations and rumours that must have been going around with the effect of Chinese whispers.

Maybe Powell's speech is not that important or related to the formation of the new BNP, as it did not emerge from the National Front until 1982 - 14 years later. However, as people still talk of Powell's speech today, I do believe that referencing Powell would have probably provided the new BNP with a good platform. Though thinking about it, if you've ever heard a John Tyndall speech then you could argue that although the BNP may reference Powell, Tyndall was convincing enough in himself to gain the support of British people. Although as previously stated, Griffin presents a more moderate viewpoint than that of Tyndall, I'm going to provide an analysis of parts of some of his speeches that I believe helps to explain why so many people are supportive of the BNP viewpoint. To avoid the argument that John Tyndall no longer represents the BNP's point of view, I will highlight where their viewpoints differ. I must, however, say that even if Griffin and newer members of the BNP have a slightly modified view from that of Tyndall, it does not mean that the older BNP members are more aligned to Griffin's viewpoint than that of Tyndall.

British Heritage and Loss of Sovereignty

England 'Til I Die
A man's t-shirt at the fish & chip shop

I believe the most dangerous lies are the lies of omission, otherwise known as half-truths. I'm talking about lies that are based on something that is real and true, but twisted to give a different meaning from that which reflects reality. Most people don't do a full analysis of half-truths. You have those who simply dismiss them as rubbish because they have sight of the bigger picture. These are often people in authority who should, however, be challenging such viewpoints, because on the other hand there are people who have a degree of trust in the speaker and/or hear the right sound bites and accept what is said as truth.

I believe that intentionally or simply by default, Nick Griffin used this tactic on Question Time when he was asked about homosexuality and men kissing, and responded that people don't want their children to see people kissing in public. I happened to be following comments on Twitter at this point in time and noticed the exasperated comment of a Labour politician who lamented, "What's he bringing children into it for?" I would venture to say that this question missed the point: Griffin had just appealed to the traditional values that a number of people in Britain still hold. Neither politician commenting on Twitter or anyone else on the panel picked up on this or even touched on the issue of values and the distinction between values and what is described as homophobia.

To be fair, politicians are generally known for telling half-truths and not answering questions directly, but I must say, John Tyndall was a true artiste.

In his 1997 speech, "Britain Falling Apart", Tyndall talked of Britain's national decline, loss of greatness, loss of strength and power, loss of capability and loss of will since the end of the First World War. He further pointed to the deterioration of quality of life in Britain that no Government seemed to have been able to stop. He goes on to blame this on government policy as opposed to being a result of war or external forces.

He went on to lament the surrender of the British Empire. He further spoke of his frustrations that while industrialisation began in Britain, almost everything, from cars, to TVs, to films, was now foreign.

If I was to simply take all of this at face value, I would possible begin to agree with him as it is true; in many ways, Britain has changed. The Britain that I was born in is very different from the Britain that I live in today - in some ways it's better, but to be honest in some ways I believe it has lost some of its essence. It is, however, very easy to romanticise the good old days. Most people for instance will think back to their school days and how good things were - we don't tend to remember the negatives. It's just the romanticisation of a first love relationship and how perfect it was.

I do, however, decry what I refer to as the de-industrialisation of Britain and believe that the move of factories to different countries in a bid for cheaper labour and production is an approach that is flawed. It is, however, part of the capitalist model that we have adopted and the subject of a whole book of itself.

It is interesting that the development of the British goes hand in hand with the British Empire as, aside from the labour, most of the resources that fuelled British industry came from the Empire countries of Africa, the West Indies and Asia. The Empire countries were also major markets for British products, so without a doubt the British Empire was of immeasurable value.

Nevertheless, while Tyndall questioned Britain's relinquishment of the Empire, I question Britain's original and ongoing rights to subjugate other peoples and their lands. The Empire arose from British colonisation of other peoples' land. I won't at this point talk about the morality of this and whether it was actually helpful and an enabler to the civilisation of the people of these lands or whether it was pure exploitation. The key point is that a time came when the people of these lands decided that they no longer wanted to be ruled by foreign occupiers such as the British and really and truly the time did arise when Britain had no real choice but to step back and relinquish what really did not belong to them in the first instance.

Considering his views on Empire, it's interesting that while Tyndall spoke of exiting from Europe and forming alliances with Canada and Australia because of their minerals and food stocks, he makes no mention of strengthening relationships with the other Commonwealth countries of Africa, Asia and the West Indies - simply because the peoples are not white.

The truth is while Tyndall spoke of Britain first and fighting for its own interest, though there is an attraction to a number of things that he said, I do not believe that what he expressed reflects the reality of the 21st century and I have not heard anything new from the BNP which constructively moves things forward.

The Defacing of the Face and Values of Britain

Haven't you noticed
A breakdown in the family tie
Just not as strong as it once was
... Bring the family back, bring it back together.
Billy Paul, Bring the Family Back

Britain has changed and will undoubtedly continue to change. There is indeed no doubt in my mind that the Britain that I live in today is very different from the Britain that I was born into and grew up in when I was small. Whether this is a good or bad thing really depends on where you stand or what side of the coin you focus on. Glass half-full or half-empty, some would say. The truth, however, is if you live in a part of Wales, the North East or North West, Birmingham or Scotland, in an area that was heavily dependent on coal mining or industry and you've watched that gradually wither away with a loss of jobs and hope for the local people, change is not going to feel good. If you live in an inner city area and you listen to the news and read the newspapers and hear constant reports about crimes and gangs, it's not going to seem good. If you are wedded to the traditional values of Britain and you hear about the high divorce rates and the changed structure of the modern British family, you are going to be concerned, if not outright alarmed, and scared that Armageddon is on our doorsteps.

John Tyndall spoke about these issues. He spoke of what used to be a stable, sturdy, morale and mainly law-abiding society which had now become a state with high crime rates and high divorce rates with family collapse. He advocated that British people wanted and needed decent places to live and work in. I suspect you, as most people, can identify with this?

Tyndall however, went on to declare the need for Britain to put its own people first; to fight for its own interest, to defend its own interest and to be a nation with pride and honour. On the face of it, I guess you could begin to agree with this. Except when the likes of Tyndall talk of Britain putting its people first, they refer to the indigenous British. If you question the concept of indigenous people, they point out that the likes of the Saxons and Vikings who migrated to Britain were white with characters and standards that were very similar to the original people of the land. Tyndall would state that blacks and Asians on the other hand are worlds apart.

They insinuate that the changes to the face of Britain are caused by multiculturalism and segregation - whereby people from black and Asian and now additionally Eastern European origins coming into the country come into certain areas in large numbers and 'force' the indigenous people to move out.

While there is a question as to how well multiculturalism has worked and how cohesive are our communities, it has done good to Britain and the presence of black and Asian people have in no way devalued British values. Statistics show that, despite the media focus on gangs in inner cities, people from ethnic minority origins are not responsible for the majority of crime in the country. Divorce rates are lower amongst ethnic minorities - most especially Asians.

Furthermore, whilst the proponents for a white, homogenous Britain could once look to Japan as a country which has a sense of its own worth, destiny and nationalism through its isolationist policies, its more recent history as reviewed later in this book show that in the global world of the 21st century, the isolation of a state or country is unsustainable.

Immigration and Immigrants

Don't pay the ferryman
Don't even fix a price
...Until he gets you to the other side
Chris De Burgh, Don't Pay the Ferryman

I will say without hesitation, that for years there have been problems with the British immigration policy if for no other reason than simply fact that there is a lack of understanding of what it is as people believe that Britain has an open border policy whereby anybody can just come in. There is also a problem about the lack of clarity as to who is actually coming in, legally or otherwise. From a business perspective I can say without warning this is wrong as it does not allow for planning. No successful business would simply put people on its payroll without knowledge of where or how they are going to be deployed and managed within the organisation. This is fact.

What is probably less clear is who is allowed to live and work within the nation and the reasoning behind it. The right-wing perspective is that people of colour should not be allowed within the country as they threaten the identity and character of Britain. Whilst the current BNP leader, Nick Griffins, speaks of voluntary deportation, Tyndall spoke of obligatory deportation of immigrants and their descendants and dependants. He cites the example of how this was achieved with the Palestinians in the Middle East and Tibetans in China. He was kind enough to acknowledge that Britain should achieve the outcome of deportation of immigrants through less brutal means. It's worth highlighting that whilst Griffins does say that deportation should be voluntary, a number of BNP bloggers/commentators seem to lean towards a more forced approach to deportation.

And from a Nick Griffin perspective, simply and plainly - stop immigration - Britain is full.

I won't say anything more about immigration, as to be really understood it needs the context of why people immigrate and specifically why people have immigrated to Britain over time. The section of this book entitled "The Legacy of an Empire" covers this in detail.

Foreign Languages, Islam ... But What About Me???

What's the charge...flying while Muslim?
Little Mosque on the Prairie

As the lady in the YouTube video "The Real BNP Supporters" outlined her concerns about the immigrant population within the UK, a man suddenly shouted out "and we wouldn't have bombers". The concern that someone would be crazy enough to strap a bomb to themselves and blow themselves up, together with as many people that they take along with them as casualties, is a real concern that no one should take lightly. Since 9/11 and enhanced by 7/7, this is a fear that people have about Muslims.

It was preceded by the prevailing fear of invasion by Islam; the fear that Muslims were going to build mosques all over the country in the place of churches and more traditional buildings and introduce Sharia law, ultimately turning Britain into an Islamic state.

I guess this fear in itself was preceded or enhanced by the frustration of next-door neighbours who covered their faces with Burga or Hijabs, of people who spoke in foreign languages and could not speak a word of English. Who at times did things differently from English-speaking people and, with the language barrier that existed, there was at times a difficulty in asking questions to understand why they do the things the way that they do.

I guess it doesn't help to make people feel better that a lot of these people don't seem interested in learning the British way of life, the language and integrating with the local people. Neither does it help that the local councils spend considerable amounts of money translating materials into different languages to accommodate such people or that the schools, specifically primary, though not exclusively so, have classes of students where considerable numbers do not speak English, such that time and resources have to be dedicated to teaching them the language.

I guess the frustration and the annoyance is worsened when statistics show that now it's increasingly white working class students that are not doing too well within the education system, when previously it was students of ethnic minority origins. I guess it's even worse that there are so many white working class people without jobs these days.

I must say if I, as a good honest citizen of this country, found myself in a position whereby my husband had been unable to find steady work for the past few years and my child wasn't doing too well in school, whilst all these other things were going on around me, I wouldn't be a happy bunny. To be honest with the best will in the world, I just might begin to resent all those foreigners that the newspapers constantly report on as coming along to take our jobs - especially those Muslims.

My fears and frustrations would be further enhanced if, when two men of Pakistani origin were found guilty and convicted of abusing young girls from Derby, a former Home Secretary and Labour MP commented in response to the case that white girls were "easy meat" to Pakistani men.

A number of the things I've mentioned are hypothetical with a basis in real life circumstances - this really did happen in January 2011 when two young men of Asian origin were found guilty and convicted of abusing young girls from Derby. In response to their conviction, Jack Straw stated that white girls (especially those from vulnerable backgrounds) were ready prey for Pakistani men who would never treat Asian girls in such a manner. His comments were made in contrast to those of the judge in the case who categorically stated that the case was not racially motivated.

But going back to me as the person who already has all the fears and concerns about Islam and Asians in the UK, I think Straw's comments and those of other people who talk without thinking of the full ramifications would most definitely make me feel justified in my fears and concerns with an urgency that I can no longer sit on the sidelines, but must do something about the situation.

If I was to look closer I would recognise that it's really not that simple. The question, however, is how much time would I take to look beyond the headlines, or would I perhaps start to have conversations with my neighbours about my grave concerns, inclusive of Bob who would explain to me that things were actually worse than I could imagine and that for the good of society and the future of my family, I like he, should join the BNP as our only hope.

A Forced Marriage of Fact and Fallacy Leading to the Conclusion

Back to Life, back to the present time
Back from a fantasy
Tell me now, take the initiative
I'll leave it in your hands until you're ready
Soul II Soul, Back to Life

I mentioned the lady in the video 'The Real BNP Supporters' who passionately defended her position as a BNP member. She pointed out that BNP supporters are British people, patriotic people - British Nationalists. She went on to talk about her family history within the origins of the Trade Unions and the fact that the BNP policies lean towards socialism and what the old Labour Party stood for. They care about the working class people and fair deal for all people without hatred for other races. Even though I don't believe this is a universal BNP perspective, I believe she was sincere about what she said.

I was, however, fascinated by her stated confusion about what she saw as barriers which favoured black people, such the Music of Black Origin (MOBO) Awards, the National Black Police Association, Black Nurses Association UK and a black education association as it would not be acceptable for white people to form similar associations without being seen as racists. Such events, organisations and associations she further saw as segregating.

I say I found this fascinating. I must confess, I also found it saddening. Saddening because she is someone whom I believe sincerely cares, who had allowed herself to get caught up and confused by populace rhetoric without viewing things in the wider context as presented by a history that she would have actually lived through.

Now don't get me wrong, there are questions as to whether the pendulum has possibly swung too far to the left, questions as to whether we have become too politically correct and as to whether there is now a need to bring an end to the groups, associations etc. that are focused on certain segments of society. But first I believe there is a need to reiterate what brought us all here and why/how the focus groups came about in the first instance.

I believe it is, however, even more difficult to reconcile the positions of groups such as the English Defence League (EDL) - a group with growing traction and some Muslim viewpoints. The EDL mission is said to be to stand up for and protect the British population against Muslim extremism, inclusive of "the denigration and oppression of women; the molestation of young children, the committing of so-called honour killings, homophobia, anti-Semitism and the continued support for those responsible for terrorist atrocities."[2] Amongst other things, they are also against Sharia law and practice within the UK and would like to see respect for the traditions and culture of England. At a basic level, when they make speeches and go on marches, it's difficult for them to demarcate between Muslim extremists and other Muslims.

---

[2] English Defence League Mission Statement from website: http://englishdefenceleague.org/about-us/mission-statement/

Indeed, Sharia has relevance to all Muslims. Furthermore, when they stand against the building of a 'super' mosque in Luton, this impacts on all Muslims in the area. However, if they believe that the building to be converted into a mosque was originally to be converted into affordable housing, things do become much more complex. The situation becomes even more complex when you take the time to listen to minority, extremist Muslim views that stereotype and condemn English ways of life and call for Sharia to be the law of the land.

It is not an easy task to reconcile the various positions and arguments, but there is a vital need to continually listen to and break down the arguments, understanding where the different parties are coming from.

The Legacy of an Empire

Original Immigrants

Dance to your Daddy, my little laddie
Dance to your Daddy, my little man
When thou art an old man, father to a son
Sing to him the old songs, sing of all you've done
Pass along the old ways, then let his song begin
Dance to your Daddy, my little man
Traditional English Folk Song, When The Boat Comes In

Whether you start from a creationist or evolutionist perspective or something in between, there is a general knowledge and acceptance that man has immigrated across the earth over time with the general thinking that man originated in Africa. If you take it as truth that we all originated from Africa then we who live here in Britain must have all migrated at some point in time. Some may, for whatever reason, attempt to dispute this or alternatively turn around and say that the first or early arrivals to Britain are the indigenous people because when they first came there was no one here, the land was without boundaries as no one had laid claim or developed the land and they who did are, therefore, the indigenous people with natural claims over the land. If you take on this argument, I'm not sure how far back you go.

Do we say that it is only those such as the Cornish, who are known to have been here possibly as far back as the Ice Age, who are the true indigenous people? Or do we include the Saxons and the Vikings, who arrived in around AD410 and AD787 respectively.

Then what about the Royal Family? After all, it is common knowledge that the Royal Family has German origins, isn't it? After all, Queen Victoria's husband, Albert, was German.

If all of the above can be accepted as indigenous people of Britain, then what about the Jacobites included blacks back in 17th century. Are they and their descendants acceptable as indigenous people? If not, on what basis do we exclude them?

I mention the above and ask the questions as, if you listen to the concerns raised about migration, you would think that it is something new to the last century that the people referred to as the indigenous people were here since the eons of time.

The truth is just as there has been extensive migration within the UK as people have moved from one place to another for better opportunities, people have migrated into and away from Britain. In many ways, such migration is a key cornerstone to the development and growth of some of the world's greatest Empires in which Britain has played a part, such as the Roman, the Ottoman and without question the British Empire, which by virtue of its name evolves around Britain.

British Empire

When a man sleeps with a woman there is a possibility that she will
get pregnant
The child that is born is as much his as hers
Susan Popoola

I was originally going to use 'Rule Britannia, Britannia Rule the Waves' as the quote for this section as really and truly the British travelled far and wider in order to establish the British Empire which overtime extended from Canada, the Caribbean and the East Coast of America, Australia, Asia and New Zealand to Africa, accounting for one third of the planet such that it was commonly said that the sun never set on the British Empire.

I believe this is well illustrated by the diagram on the next page, which, while not showing all of Britain's colonies and territories, does highlight the fact that there was at least one in each of the time zones.

With dominion over a third of the world and with such a major spread, it's not a major exaggeration to say that Britain once ruled the world. But I suspect that everyone knows this, don't they? So you may wonder why I'm even bothering to mention it, most especially as it could be said to reinforce the frustrations and concerns of those who wish for a return of Britain's glory days.

Well I mention it because while, yes it's true - Britain once had something remarkable in the British Empire, whether or not you

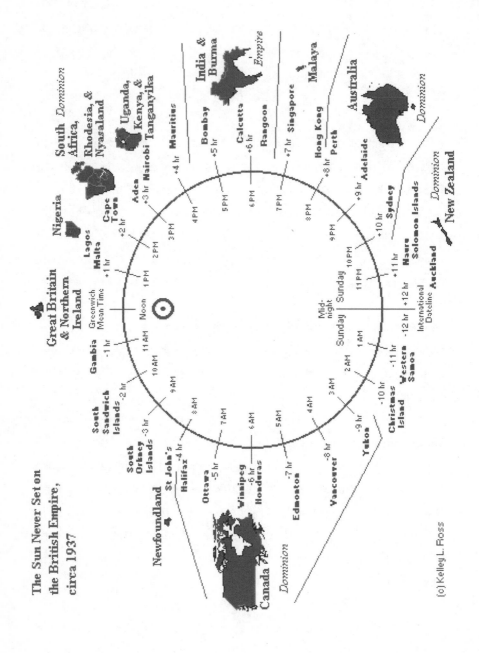

The Sun Never Set on the British Empire, circa 1937

(c) Kelley L. Ross

56

believe that it had a right to it - it gave most of it up not because it wanted to, but because circumstances and world events dictated. There was, however, a lot that happened within the timeframe of acquisition and the eventual relinquishment of territories. The impact varied from one territorial area or colony to another, but the Britain of today is largely a consequence of the British Empire as a significant number of the people in Britain today, who are typically referred to as immigrants, have a link to Britain from Britain's colonial days.

You see, for the most part Britain adopted a philosophy of indirect rule to run its territories. This meant that it gave them a fair amount of autonomy to run themselves using the systems already in place, but putting systems in place to enable Britain's management of the territories where the Colonial Power felt the systems in existence did not work. At the same time, Britain took on a paternal role, with the expectation that it would be called upon for major decisions. This was especially so in the Americas. The same was largely applied in Africa and Asia, though the British did get more involved especially as related to cultural activities that they found abhorrent. They also had the tendency to use the traditional systems already in place to implement British systems. If you go to a number of former British colonies in Africa today, you will find that they still, for instance, operate a modified version of the British legal structure. As such, a number of these countries even today have systems in place that are common with those in Britain.

Beyond the economic and financial relationships that existed and still largely exist, English was imported across the territories and became the national language of most countries, creating a further bond. Britain was set up as and looked up to as the motherland, as is still largely the case today. This is reflected in ongoing economic and political relationships. Most overtly it is reflected in the existence of the Commonwealth of Nations which consists of a number of former British colonies. When the Commonwealth was set up, it was headed by the Queen of England as it still is today.

To further emphasise the impact of Britain on the world, during the reign of Queen Elizabeth I (1558-1603), the number of English speakers in the world is thought to have been between five and seven million. By the tenure of Queen Elizabeth II, over three centuries later, this amount has increased almost five fold.

In addition to the official title of The Head of The Commonwealth, Queen Elizabeth is also the monarch and head of state for 15 other sovereign states outside of the United Kingdom inclusive of Antigua and Barbuda; Australia; Bahamas, Barbados; Belize; Canada; Grenada; Jamaica; New Zealand; Papua New Guinea; Saint Kitts and Nevis; Saint Lucia; Saint Vincent and Grenadines; Solomon Islands and Tuvalu.

Selah, i.e. pause and ponder.

North Americas and Australia

On the boats and on the planes
They're coming to America
Never looking back again
They're coming to America
Neil Diamond, America

You know that special relationship between the USA and Britain that was often spoken about by Tony Blair in terms of US/UK relationships? The relationship that I would say led people to cruelly refer to Blair as George Bush's puppy. Well, there is a good historical reason for it. After all, the US was one of Britain's very first colonies and the Americans have not forgotten this. I believe it's one of the reasons when I visit the States that I'm frequently told by Americans that us British speak proper English. Possibly more pertinent to the connection is the present day Tea Party movement which derives its name from the Boston Tea Party, the landmark for the US's fight for independence from Britain. Furthermore, World War II was said to have been won largely on account of the US intervention and involvement, which further strengthens the connection.

I don't know if you've visited the US before, but even without paying a visit if you take a good look at a map of the United States, you may be surprised to find how many places in the States are named after British towns. For instance, if in England you say Birmingham, you'd be referring to a place in the Midlands. However, if Americans say Birmingham they would be referring to a place in the State of Alabama. Then in America you also have places with names such as Billerica, Chelmsford, Dorchester, Cambridge, Plymouth, Uxbridge, Dartmouth, Gloucester, Falmouth, New London, New Bedford, Attenborough, Kingston and Dedham. The same can also be found in parts of Canada (part of Canada was once British territory) and Australia.

Beyond names, there are good links between these countries and Britain, with British citizens being able to visit most of these countries without having to apply for visa (and vice versa)[3]. Though this does not apply to working visas or permits and people from such countries are now impacted by the British immigration point system, I don't recall people complaining about Americans, Australians or Canadians coming into the UK.

Without question, as even the far-right would admit, I believe this is because the majority of immigrants and visitors from these countries are of European origin, as from pre-colonial days to the present, these are primary countries that British citizens tend to have migrated to, settled in and formed the majority of the populations. This is, of course, aside from the relatively smaller numbers that now tend to be migrating to countries such as Spain, though this, more often than not, is for retirement or semi-retirement.

---

[3]British Citizens do need a visa to go to Australia

Asia

We have ... fought for our place in the sun and have won it
Emperor Wilhelm II 1897-1941

Many believe that the arrival in Britain of people from the Indian subcontinent began in the 1950s, in response to the demand for post-war labour. There was in fact a significant influx at this stage.

However, way back in the 17th century, British families returning from India brought over with them Indian servants and nannies via sail vessels or later steamboats. In fact some European men actually returned to Britain with Indian wives and children. Asian teachers also came to Britain to teach oriental languages. Some of these people were eventually returned to India when no longer required, but an unknown number remained in British homes.

From about the middle of the 19th century, an increasing number of Indians - largely professionals - came to Britain. Some came as a result of the political, social and economic changes brought about under colonial rule. Others came out of a sense of adventure or curiosity to see the land of their rulers, or as in the case of the princes, on official visits or for pleasure. Students, some on scholarships, came to obtain vital professional qualifications to enable them to gain entry into the structures of colonial hierarchy back home. Some, having qualified, stayed on to practise their professions in Britain.

By the end of the Second World War, several thousand Asians had been living in Britain for generations and an 'Asian community' was already in existence. There were Asian professionals, industrial workers and labourers, students and activists, petty traders, merchants and businessmen, artists and writers. Asians, then (as now), were not a homogenous community.

There was an additional influx of Asians who came into Britain from East Africa in the 1960s as a result of movements towards Africanism and nationalism that came alongside post colonial independence in Africa. The consequences of this on Asians were most apparent under Idi Amin's Uganda.

Taking account of all of this, it's really no surprise that our family doctor, when I lived in South London back in the 1990s, was Dr Patel. He had been the family doctor for many, many years prior to this. At first I was surprised to find out that our family doctor was not the only Dr Patel around. Do a Google search of the name and you will see what I mean. I still remember Dr Fletcher, our family doctor in the 1970s, who was ever so kind and reassuring to me when I swallowed a boiled sweet and thought I was going to die at the tender age of six. However, there is a reality that whilst many are today concerned about the future of the NHS due to the plans of the coalition government, the organisation would not exist without all the doctors who came from places such as India to work in the NHS (together with the nurses typically from the Caribbean). The NHS is a lot more diverse now, but we are getting to a point where a lot of those doctors who came from different countries to serve us will be retiring - I only hope we have done the succession planning in order to be able to fill the gap that will be created.

Asians have not just come to Britain to serve in the NHS though, a lot of them came into retail and made a marked impact in this area - though let's be honest, to many it has been a hard experience to see a number of corner shops being taken over by Asians.

An interesting thing about Asian immigrants, as most immigrants, is that they are typically not those with the lowest income and employment opportunities in their home countries, but rather they tend to be those with the resources, education skills and experience that makes them employable in the country of immigration. This, coupled with the fact that people who take the risk of migrating to another country are often quite entrepreneurial in their thinking, also accounts for why immigrants to Britain may often succeed where long-term residents may not.

The Caribbean

They came to England because there are gold nuggets on the floor,
they actually found that there was dark stuff on the floor
and they had to clean it up
Windrush. The Irresistible Rise of Multi-Racial Britain
Phillips & Phillips

As you would probably know even if I hadn't mentioned it, the Empire Windrush docked at Tilbury in 1948. After there have been numerous documentaries and books written that talk about the Windrush, I believe it is also now included in school curriculums. There had been a trickle of arrivals from the Caribbean prior to this, but the arrival of the Windrush has gone down in history as a key demarcation of the beginning of the arrival of people from the Caribbean to Britain.

To the people on that boat, as to many who came after, it was a journey to the motherland. In many ways, just as people today move within the country, typically from the North to the South or from small towns and villages to large cities and towns, in search of better opportunities and ultimately a better life, so did people travel from the Caribbean to Britain.

At times there are limited opportunities in small towns and villages and people are told about all the opportunities in the big towns. It's a natural step for people to move to the towns. The move from the Caribbean to Britain was actually just as natural as, although Britain and the British Caribbean were not one country, they were in the first instance all part of the British

Empire which could be seen as one entity under British rule. Even with the fall of the British Empire, Britain kept close links with its Caribbean colonies under the auspices of the Commonwealth so, for a long time, Britain remained the motherland to the people of the Caribbean.

In the early stages, migration to Britain was encouraged due to shortages in the UK labour market. A lot of people within the Caribbean had limited opportunities and with an education based on the British education system, when Britain advertised for and encouraged the people to come to Britain - where there were said to be ample opportunities and a need for help in rebuilding post-war - an estimated quarter of a million Afro-Caribbean people arrived to settle permanently in Britain between 1955 and 1962. This migration was, however, suddenly limited by new immigration legislation in the 1960s.

The thing is, people from the Caribbean didn't come to Britain as immigrants, or blacks, but as sibling Britons, who knew their way around the formal curriculum of Britain as well as any other Britons.

Africa

Teacher Don't Teach Me Nonsense
Fela Kuti

In many ways Britain was the motherland for people from Britain's colonies in Africa as well. Education in Britain's colonies in Africa was also based on the British education system. Africans, and specifically Nigerians, are known to place a very high value on education. However, the first Nigerian university was not established until 1948 - this was the University of Ibadan which was originally established as an independent external college of the University of London. The first fully indigenous university was the University of Nigeria which was not established until 1960, with a number of other universities subsequently established through the following decade.

It is only natural that people seeking university education went elsewhere and Britain - the motherland or the seat of the Empire - was the natural place for Nigerians to go to. In fact until today, Nigerians who choose to send their children or obtain education outside of Nigeria typically come to Britain, even though they may now alternatively go to other places such as America as well.

I live in Milton Keynes, which aspires to have a university with a specific focus on local people. A key reason for this is because, as it currently stands, whether they like it or not, students who go to secondary school in Milton Keynes who want to go on to university have to go outside of Milton Keynes for that part of their education, and a significant number of them find work in the area in which they went to university and don't come back to Milton Keynes - at least not for some time.

The same applied to many of the Nigerians and other Africans who came to Britain for their education. In many ways, a number of them became more ingrained in Britain because, due to the fact that they were going to be in England for a number of years, if they had children back at home, when the opportunity arose they naturally sent for their children to come and live with them. Others and some of the same, had children whilst they were living here in England. Although a significant number of students from Africa came to England on scholarships, they largely worked whilst in school which further embedded them in Britain.

There were also people from African countries who came to Britain to work or simply gain the experience of living within the British environment. Some people wanted their children to gain a British education as, from the experiences and the information they received from Britons living in Africa (especially during the colonial period), they had come to the understanding that this was the best place for their children to be educated.

When people protest against immigration, they often complain against the number of foreign students in Britain. What they miss out when they make these complaints is that before the recent increase in tuition fees, foreign students paid fees which were typically at least twice as high as those paid by British students - they therefore help to subsidise the system. By staying in the UK for a period after finishing their studies, if nothing else, they are making some degree of contribution to the British economy by their tax contributions, even if they do send a significant proportion of their earnings back home.

There is also something of a reversal in some cases, whereby many Nigerians born in England in the 1950s, 60s and 70s were taken to Nigeria by their parents when they were quite young, went to school in Nigeria and then came back for their university education - just as their parents did. Alternatively, they may have completed their university education in Nigeria and then come back to Britain for a post-graduate qualification, or simply to work, and they have every right to do so as they are in effect British citizens.

With the ties built from the colonial period, further enhanced via the Commonwealth, African countries and their indigenes retain strong ties with Britain.

Over the years, problems in Africa have led to the further migration of Africans to Britain. Specifically, there has been the migration of people from countries such as Somalia and Zimbabwe due to problems of famine, civil war and dictatorial Governments; African Asians from Uganda due to the expulsion by Idi Amin; and white Africans from South Africa after the end of apartheid, specifically with the refocus of the country on trying to address the historical imbalances by trying to provide opportunities for black South Africans.

To and From The Continent i.e. Europe

The great nations of Europe coming through
Randy Newman, The Great Nations of Europe

Historically the vast majority of long-term and permanent migration in relation to Britain was linked to the British Empire. This has now changed a fair amount - partly due to circumstances in other parts of the world, which have meant that there are a number of people who have migrated to Britain on an asylum or refugee basis. This is muddied by the case of illegal immigrants from different places. We will come back to this, but for now I'd like to talk about Europe.

There are ongoing debates as to whether or not it was a good thing for Britain to join the European Union and there are arguments both ways relating to the impact on industry, legislation and so many other things. For now, I just want to focus in on how this has impacted on migration.

Most frequently, we talk of this in the negative. Focusing on how people from Eastern European countries, such as Poland, have come in and taken away jobs from British workers, most especially as they are often willing to work for lower wages, often beneath the minimum wage. This does not question why employers would take the illegal action of employing people below the minimum wage and place responsibility with them or government. It would, however, say that it does rightly question government policy and preparedness.

But of equal importance, these arguments neglect to acknowledge how a number of British citizens have benefited from the Union as there are a fair number of Britons who have either out rightly moved to countries such as Spain or Cyprus - specifically for retirement. There are others still who work in such countries with a number of others living in other parts of Europe and commuting to work in Britain with the aid of the Eurotunnel and cheap air flights. They would not have been so enabled to make such choices prior to the advent of the European Union. So whilst some may feel that they have suffered for it, others have undoubtedly benefited.

Globalisation - Two-edged Sword

Did you think I'd leave you dying
When there's room on my horse for two
Climb up here Joe, we'll soon be flying
I can go just as fast with two
... I think it's that I remember when we were two little boys
Rolf Harris, Two Little Boys

It is a basic fact that today's Britain is very different from the Britain of the 70s, 80s and even 90s - it's changed and you don't have to be a rocket scientist to have worked that out. However, whether you see the new and future emerging Britain as good or bad may depend as much on what side of the table you are sitting on as whether you are a 'cup half-full' or 'half-empty' kind of person.

At a basic level, Britain has changed because it has always been evolving and with the passage of time it has become more apparent; it's the way of the world - that is how we develop and improve. At another level, it has changed because the rest of the world has done so and in as much as Britain may be an island, it is not viable for it to operate in isolation.

European (not just British) exploration and colonisation of most parts of the world invariably opened the world up - first and foremost to the benefit of Europe and European trade. Exploration then spreading further afield to the Americas, Asia and other parts of the world with decolonisation. It's not a level playing field, but Britain does have historical advantages and as a result competitive advantages that, though not as strong as they used to be, are still in existence.

To compete effectively, even though Britain has maintained most of its historical alliances, it has also had to build new ones - a key reason for membership of the European Union, whether you agree with it or not.

Changes had to be made with the way in which British industry was run - some changes were inevitable due to advances in technology and resource requirements, but were unpopular in their implementation such as those changes within the coal industry. Changes were often made to ensure profitability, such as the move of factories to other countries where production is cheaper, often without due consideration for the impact on local workers and communities.

It's the global world that we all now live in which comes with opportunities, challenges and responsibilities which at times compete with each other. These opportunities may lead the most daring to relocate to where the opportunities exist. This, however, comes alongside the recognition that migration of workers into an area may impact on jobs for local people, but more often than not does not, as new arrivals often come with skills that are not available locally. At the same time, however, these workers are coming with skills that may be critically required in the workers' home country - I'm talking about the phenomenon called brain drain.

It's on account of the perceived need to manage this movement by excluding and including people as deemed appropriate, that different governments over the years have implemented varying immigration policies. The truth be known, for most, Britain is still as it has long been: a good place to live in, and thus holds an attraction for many outside, especially in less developed parts of the world.

If you trace back on government policy, you will see that the policy has not always been to exclude - sometimes with the recognition of gaps within the UK workforce, it has been aimed at including. Take a look at the British immigration legislation over the years since 1948:

- 1948 Nationality Act: gave rights of entry and citizenship to all citizens of British colonies and the Commonwealth.
- 1962 Commonwealth Immigrants Act: introduced 'entry vouchers' for Commonwealth citizens, issued on the basis of skills and qualifications. Entry was on the basis of a, b or c:
  a. have a job to come to;
  b. possess special skills which were in short supply; or,
  c. be a part of a large undifferentiated group whose numbers would be set according to the labour needs of the United Kingdom economy.
- 1968 Commonwealth Immigrants Act: distinguished between UK passport holders with a right of abode, partials - those born or naturalised in UK or with a UK born grandparent, and those without.
- 1971 Immigration Act: set out the structure of immigration control and gave power to the Home Secretary to make

immigration rules. All those without a right of abode were required to seek work permit. This Act also introduced the end of primary migration from the Commonwealth (though this continued in shortage skills areas).

- 1981 British Nationality Act: those qualifying for a right of abode were given British citizenship. Children born in Britain of non-British citizens lost an automatic right to citizenship.
- 1987 Immigration (Carriers' Liability) Act: introduced fines on airlines carrying passengers without the correct documents.
- 1988 Immigration Act: made deportation easier; withdrew the right of family reunion from Commonwealth men; and established a 'primary purpose' marriage rule.
- 1993 Asylum and Immigration Appeals Act: incorporated the Geneva Convention into immigration rules, creating processes for dealing with asylum applications. This piece of legislation also withdrew the right of appeal for visitors and students.
- 1996 Asylum and Immigration Act: withdrew non-contributory benefits for asylum seekers and other groups subject to immigration control, for example work permit holders.
- 1999 Asylum and Immigration Act: created the National Asylum Support Service (NASS) system for asylum seekers; created a single appeal stage; imposed a duty on marriage registrars to report suspicious marriages; strengthened powers of immigration officers in enforcing controls; extended carrier sanctions; and imposed regulation on immigration advice.
- 2002 Nationality, Immigration and Asylum Act: introduced new controls on entry; a new citizenship pledge; and

limited the powers of Immigration Appeals Tribunals to hear appeals on human rights grounds.

- 2004 Asylum and Immigration (Treatment of Claimants etc.) Act: introduced new system of appeals with Asylum and Immigration Tribunals; created a criminal offence of entering the UK without a valid passport. A Certificate of Approval from the Secretary of State was also required for marriages involving a person requiring leave to remain.
- 2006 Immigration, Asylum and Nationality Act: increased grounds for depriving dual nationals of citizenship; reduced rights to appeals and increased the role of employers in preventing 'illegal' working.
- 2009 Borders, Citizenship and Immigration Act: introduced a five tiered points system which focused on ensuring that workers from overseas were only employed within the UK when there is a specific requirement for their skills.

Moving on from the actual immigration, problems in other places in the world such as Uganda, Vietnam (the Boat People), Iraq (The Kurds) and the Balkans (following the breakup of Yugoslavia) have also led to waves of migration. Britain has a moral responsibility to respond to the needs of asylum seekers and refugees.

Although there is an anomaly in asylum seekers, in more general terms it can be argued that the pattern of immigration and settlement of Commonwealth citizens closely matched the pattern of demand in the labour market in the past. There is still a deep connection that makes Britain a destination of choice for Commonwealth citizens.

Bearing in mind the above and the consequences of history, I would venture to say it is too simplistic to simply say that Britain has not done enough to protect its borders as far as immigration goes. Whilst I believe that more should have been done to understand who was coming in and why, I believe Britain is faced with a conundrum as far as immigration is concerned as a consequence of history.

So Let's Really And Honesty Talk About Race

Superior and Inferior Races

We people who are darker than blue
Are we gonna stand around this town
And let what others say come true?
We're just good for nothing they all figure
Curtis Mayfield, We The People Who Are Darker Than Blue

It's difficult to say precisely when the notion of white superiority begun or why it came about, but it has existed and though the message is now more subtle, except with outright racists groups and people, the notion persists.

Some will trace back in the Bible to the story of Noah when he cursed one of his sons, Shem. Such people will say that Africans are the descendants of Shem, who are cursed and therefore a lesser people. This is a viewpoint typically expressed by some Christians. The ironic part of it, is that regardless of all the imagery, there is no way in which Jesus living in the Middle East would have been white.

Others will trace back to the beginning of the colonial period when the British first went to Africa and Asia. They will talk about the inferior ways of life of the people and how they were actually helped by British colonisation which helped to develop them. People may refer to the indigenous peoples as savages and refer to customs that may have existed in a few, minute areas such as the killing of twins which, by all accounts was wrong, but was not widespread. The truth of the matter, however, is that some of the things that may be condemned or cited as examples of backwardness may have taken place in Britain not too many years earlier.

On the contrary to these opinions, history does however demonstrate well-developed cultures and ways of life in Africa and Asia - some will say that civilisation actually begun in Africa as evidenced by Egyptian civilisation. But those who want to believe differently will dispute this so much so that I recently saw an argument that stated that there were/may have been white mummies - showing photos of mummies with what seemed to be red hair.

I'd like to say "who cares, it doesn't matter anymore", but sadly the truth is that it does matter because many people still maintain the beliefs of superior and inferior relationships that affect the way in which they interact with people who they see as different.

I don't think it helps that whenever Africa or parts of Asia, such as India, are shown on television, more often than not, you are likely to see pictures of the slums and poorest parts of the countries which would equate to television portraying Britain from the perspective of its most deprived areas as if that was the totality of Britain.

The interesting thing is when Britain is portrayed most of the time the very best of Britain is shown whilst the worst of Africa is shown. With this, it's therefore not surprising that when you talk of Africa, people who have not visited have a very limited and negative viewpoint. There is a general lack of awareness that many of the Africans that you see in Britain have very ostentatious life styles in their home countries that many British people wouldn't even dream of. I would venture to say that the same applies to Asia.

All of this encourages people to make statements such as "they are different from us" or "they have different values from us". The subtlety of the message as portrayed today is also reflected in the limited expectations that people often have of the abilities of people of colour.

But are they really different? I mean, at this point in time - who is really the "we" and who is "they", after we've all been living together for so long?

Institutional Racism

Police and thieves in the streets
Oh yeah!
Fighting the nation with their guns and ammunition
Junior Murvin, Police and Thieves

Does the name Stephen Lawrence ring a bell? For most people it will. If you're black and living in Britain, it must!

You see, Stephen Lawrence was a young college boy who was attacked by about five white guys for no other reason than the colour of his skin. I think it would be fair to say that the investigation was not handled properly - race played a part in this too. I can say this without hesitation as the lack of prosecution (in spite of the fact that the perpetrators of the crime were known) and the struggles of Stephen's parents for justice led to the Stephen Lawrence inquiry. A key fact that came out from the investigation was that there was institutional racism within the police system.

It's now over 10 years since the results of the inquiry were published so the hope would be that the problems have been rectified within the police system and that other British institutions would have used the learnings from the inquiry to get rid of racism within their own institutions. But have they?

Beyond this, the sad reality is that whether real or imagined, the general belief that it still exists will take a very long time to disappear from our minds, as exemplified by the following story.

Before I say anything else, I must say that this is quite sensitive, but at the same time it is the type of thing that causes a lot of concern, so it must be spoken about - though with as much sensitivity as possible.

On the 17th December 2010, Joanna Yeates, a 25 year old living in Bristol, was reported missing. It was all across the news and subsequently in the newspapers. Sadly, a body was discovered on Christmas Day and it was later reported to be Jo's body - she had been strangled. A murder investigation was launched; her landlord was arrested for questioning; the driver of a 4x4 was wanted for questioning; it was stated that two people may have been involved in the murder. Police involved in a murder investigation in Bedford 30 years ago were involved. I picked all this up from snippets of the news reported on an almost daily basis. I felt very, very sad for the parents and her boyfriend thinking that life, and most especially Christmas, would never, ever be the same for them. At the same time, I must confess that I did wonder why this particular case was receiving so much attention, after all it is reported that approximately 600 people go missing each day.[4]

I wondered further what criteria the police use to determine what stories they are going to highlight when a friend reported on Twitter on the 4th January that a 14 year old named Serena Beakhurst went missing on the 15th December. Looking into this story I read that the police allegedly refused to use the media in the

---

[4]Duncan Campbell. Have You Seen Our Son. The Guardian. Thursday 9th March 2006

case as they thought she might be a runaway. There were, however, a few celebrities, including Stephen Fry, Rio Ferdinand and Sarah Brown (wife of ex-Prime Minister Gordon Brown) amongst other people, who had used social media to highlight the case, such that it was on a section on the BBC website and the Voice, amongst other newspapers.

Reading remarks from commentators on the Voice online:

"Two females go missing two days apart one black, working class from Brixton the other white middle class from an affluent area equals two different responses? It's shameful that in this day and age the British media continues to send the message that some life has more value than others."

"The mainstream media refuses to give coverage to Serena who is STILL missing but continues to give maximum coverage to Joanna Yeates who has already been found?"

"Why is it that the disappearance of a white middle class female becomes front page news, whilst that of a 14 year old mixed race girl from a working class family does not even raise a glimmer of attention?"

Was it institutional racism - I don't know. I hope not, but to be honest it does seem unfair and I must say it does allow for what are probably, or at least hopefully, misconceptions.

The great thing is that on the 5th of January, I learnt that Serena had been found - alive and well. Unfortunately the details of the incident were not released to the public.

The question therefore still remained as to what criteria the police use to determine what cases they are going to highlight and give national coverage to. At the very least, in order to get rid of the notion of institutional racism, I believe there is a need for more openness about the criteria that the police and other British institutions use to make decisions.

Is It Because I is Black? The Race Card

Is it Because I Is Black?
Ali G

One of the key issues with institutional racism as with racism more generally, is the impact that it has on black and Asian people beyond direct discrimination, whereby people often have an expectation of how white people are going to behave, treat them or respond to them. This was illustrated to me by an interview that I saw with Bonnie Greer, an American author, playwright and long-term resident in the UK. During the interview she mentioned the fact that, because she grew up in segregated America, whenever she is walking and sees that there is a white lady walking in front of her, she makes sure that she walks in a way that enables the white lady to have a proper view of her. She said she does this to ensure that the white lady doesn't get the impression that she is trying to take anything from her bag. Why should this be if not for the conditioning based on her past? The flip side of this is when, due to past experiences and/or the experiences of others, a victim mentality is developed, whereby individuals of colour come to believe that when things go wrong or just don't work out for them they have been victimised because of the colour of their skin.

There is a reality that people of colour are disproportionately stopped and searched. Similarly with all the legislation in place, there is still a reality that people of colour are disadvantaged in the workplace and under-represented at senior levels, either due to current practices as there are people who will still favour white people over people of colour for jobs.

I still remember a conversation that I had with a recruitment manager within an organisation a few years back. She had worked with another manager on the shortlist for the position of his new PA. They had shortlisted three candidates with one candidate, let's call her Shirley Brown, standing out above the other candidates. During the interviews as far as the recruitment manager was concerned, Shirley remained the top candidate, but suddenly the other manager started finding faults with her that didn't really exist. Talking to the recruitment manager, there was only one reason that she could find to explain the other manager's change of heart and that was the simple fact that, although you couldn't tell from Shirley's name, she happened to be mixed race. He therefore didn't want her to work as his PA.

This is a much more subtle response than that which my brother received about 20 years back when he had a telephone interview for a job which was virtually offered to him. When he went in to the office, the manager looked at him in shock and told him that from his surname, Popoola, he thought he was Greek. My brother didn't get the job.

There is also the reality that even with the passage of time and the aid of positive discrimination programmes, it still takes time for people to progress up the ladders within organisations.

The situation is not, however, helped when there are problems with people's performance at work and they are not informed, but instead sidelined. As with anyone, the person in question is more likely than not to jump to the wrong conclusions about the situation.

On the other hand, there is a different reality that sometimes people do take things to an extreme, whereby everything bad that happens to them is attributed to racism.

I used to watch the X-Factor and its predecessor shows on a regular basis. After the show I would often compare notes with a few friends. I have a friend, Trevor, who would always complain when a black contestant who was quite good was voted off the show. Jokingly, we would say "it's the racists, she or he was much better than all of those other contestants". I would ask him whether he voted for the contestant to which he would always respond by saying "is s/he going to pay me?". I'd smile and say "well, there you go" and that would end the conversation. In this case it was a joke that we shared, but it does actually reflect what a number of people do actually believe. It's a form of a victim's mentality which is unfortunate because it can be destructive and hold people back. This does not, however, mean that at times it is not justifiable.

Living in Rome

'Do at Rome as the Romans do,' is the essence of all politeness
E. Howard (1836) Rattlin, The Reefer I. xxii.

There's an old saying - 'when in Rome do as the Romans do'. To a significant extent, I believe this should be applicable to living in Britain, but in other ways it's somewhat hypocritical and difficult to justify. Let me explain.

I've heard people say that the British don't have any culture. I will say categorically that this is not true - they do have a very strong culture and ethic, even if it is evolving over time, just as culture does everywhere.

I believe when you go into a country (as with a company), you should take the time to gain an understanding of the culture and interact with it. To my mind, that includes taking the time to learn the language such that you're not in a position whereby you have lived in a country for years and can't speak the language.

I say this with the understanding that you may speak your native language at home, but that you are still able to interact with others outside in English. You take the time to understand the way in which people do things and why. This does not mean that you have to go to a pub and drink alcohol if you are against drinking it. You may possibly go to the pub but drink something else - unless you just can't bear to see other people drinking.

On the other hand, I'm conscious that there has been an issue of acceptance for people of colour, such that they were typically not accepted in churches, with white people often leaving when a number of black people came in. This lead to circumstances whereby black people were often compelled to form their own churches.

It's not only in churches, but typically when people of colour start moving into an area, it's not universal practice, but some local people in the past have been known to move out of areas because of new arrivals, not giving the new arrivals the real opportunity to integrate with them as I believe they should.

I do, however, say this with the consciousness that this does not reflect how British people typically have behaved in the past when they have colonised. In fact, rather than taking the time to understand the cultures of the indigenous people, the colonial power has viewed their cultures from a simplistic perspective, declaring them primitive and inferior - imposing British culture and ways of life with impunity.

Even today, the typical British person abroad has the tendency to go to non-British people and speak English at them, expecting them to understand and respond in English, showing our frustration by speaking slowly so that the person in question will understand, without even making an attempt to try and speak the language of the indigenous people of the country that we are visiting.

Shades of Grey Mean It's Too Late to go Back

My Identity

One life is all we have to live, our love is all we have to give.
The SOS Band, Take Your Time (Do It Right)

Many moons ago, I volunteered as a youth worker. Through my interactions with the young people I picked up some street lingua. I found that one of ways of breaking down some barriers with them was to speak a bit of 'street' to them. The result was always the same. They would look at me horrified and laugh because it didn't quite sound right. After the laughter they seemed to relax and feel more at ease talking to me. I was recently reminded of this when I bumped into someone I worked with about five years ago. Above everything else, he remembered and reminded me of an incident that took place in the office one Friday afternoon. Everyone was sat back relaxed, chatting away as we worked. Just for the fun of it, I decided to speak a bit of 'street'. I uttered a few lines of my broken 'street' and the guy looked up at me with a look of shock on his face and, without thinking, he uttered, "Susan, you sound like a white person trying to be black", to which everyone burst out laughing. I laughed as well, but it does actually lead up to the question of my identity.

I don't often talk about this, but when I was small, I didn't actually live with my biological parents. I was privately fostered and lived together with two of my older sisters with my mum (a white lady) and her daughter. It might sound strange but it was actually quite common in those days. In fact, a friend recently showed me a book about the process which actually has examples of adverts which were placed in newspapers by Nigerian parents.

My original explanation for this taking place is that from the 1950s specifically through to the 70s, a lot of young Nigerians came to England - the motherland - to study. Some came married, others got married while they were here and as you would naturally expect, a number of them had children. If they had been at home, they would have had support from their extended families (specifically parents) in looking after/bringing up their children as they were studying and working around the clock. My theory is that in the absence of the extended family, they found white ladies to look after their children for them.

Regardless of the reasoning, it happened and, though to a lesser extent and under much better regulation and management, it still takes place today. I first became aware that this was still taking place about 10 years ago when I watched a programme on telly about it. A Nigerian family had a child fostered with a British family in Wales. For whatever reasons, a family friend of the biological family was asked to go and collect the child from Wales. During the train journey back to London, the child started crying. The family friend tried to comfort her by singing to the child in a Nigerian language; the child responded by singing a song in Welsh.

In case you are to say, well, that was 10 years ago; I was at an exhibition about a year ago and happened to get into a conversation with a lady from a local council fostering and adoption department. She reiterated to me that private adoption is still very much a regular practice.

The impact of this is that until I was about eight, when my sisters and I were taken to Nigeria, I was brought up as a white person - with brown skin. I didn't realise it at the time and although I know from my sisters that we did suffer some degree of racial abuse, I was possibly too young to have a clear memory of this beyond being called chocolate drops by a friend, to whom I remember responding by calling her white chocolate.

When I was eight, my parents took my sisters and I 'home' to Nigeria. The truth, however, is that for me it didn't feel like home and the people didn't treat me as one of them. Rather because I spoke and behaved differently, they referred to me as "oyinbo" - English person. I would venture to say that a number of people of Nigerian origin born in Britain have moved to Nigeria, integrated and felt at home there, but many more (based on the conversations that I have had) like I, never felt at home. In fact, even people born in countries such as Nigeria, who then come to live in England for an extended period of time, often find it difficult to reintegrate to the country of their birth. As a consequence for me, whilst I was in Nigeria, I always had the desire to come back home to England and as soon as I had the opportunity to do so, I came back.

The interesting thing for me now is the question that other people raise with me from time to time as to what my identity is when I'm asked by Nigerians. I know that whilst I wasn't fully accepted as Nigerian when I lived there, they expect me to say I'm Nigerian. I therefore respond by saying that my parents were Nigerian (they've now passed away). At times this does not seem to satisfy them as they sort of sneer at me and saying, so what are you? You can never be English. I used to try and explain to them that I'm not saying that I'm English - rather I'm British. At times, I would then get a sad look as I was told that I'm lost.

The interesting thing is that most other people don't seem to ask or accept that I'm British, whilst older people may inquire further to which I inform them that I originate from Nigeria. More often than not, this satisfies them.

These days I tend to give different responses to suit my audience and avoid a big debate. I know and can unashamedly state that there is a part of me that is Nigerian, but also a part of me that is very British. I recognise that this may not be appreciated, but I feel quite mixed, but ultimately for me personally, I'm simply Susan. The key reason why I mention this is because, with all the programmes and books that I've seen and read respectively on Empire and Black Britain, I believe that I represent two (interrelated) groups of people in Britain that are very rarely spoken of, i.e. black people who are brought up as white and the British born black person who is in some ways also an immigrant.

I know that I'm not the only one who has faced this dilemma so I'd be interested to know, what do you think, am I British, Nigerian, a British African, African Briton or what? And does it actually matter to you?

Ok, Truly Mixed Race

Girl, who are you? It's a strange thing
I can't find you, you're always changing
You're a secret I wished that I knew, you're so distant but what can I do?
Every day of my life, I'm looking for you
The Dukes, Mystery Girl

Though I might feel quite mixed at times and describe myself to close friends as a mashed up person - as I've just taken what I hope is the best of all the different cultures and ways of life that I have encountered over time and inculcated them to become who I am - the truth, however, is that I'm not mixed race - I'm black.

There are, however, an increasing number of people in Britain who are mixed and who actually see it as a good thing.

You see I love walking - I always have. I was therefore walking through Stockgrove Country Park one Saturday afternoon when I came across a family having a picnic. There was a little girl of about four merrily chatting away. I didn't hear what she said, but I gently smiled when I heard her father respond, "Are you going to marry an African prince and add a little colour to the family?"

Now this would be readily accepted by most people. People wouldn't give her and her African prince strange looks as they walk along the road as she would be one of many, and, most important of all, she's unlikely to have abuse rained on her. Similarly her children wouldn't go to school and stand out as odd, even if they may at times struggle with their identity. Are they black? No one would call them white, even if their upbringing led them to feel that way.

It's not like the days when it was taboo for a white person to be seen with a black person, most especially a white lady with a black man. It's not even like the 1980s when Lenny Henry and Dawn French (amongst others) got married and were prime targets for hate campaigns by racists.

These days, mixed race relationships are commonplace. This is reflected in **986,600** of the population who identified themselves as mixed race in 2009. An increase of coming close to 50% from 672,000 figure of 2001. Haringey in North London is actually reported to have the highest proportion of **4.4%** mixed race.[5] You only need to look around you at young people to see that this trend is on the increase.

Mixed race relations and families have become even more complex as well. It's no longer just about black and white or even white and Asian. It's now black and Asian and all the other combinations you could possibly think of. My godson's mum is British-Australian, whilst his dad is Japanese.

I remember attending a Black History Month event at a government department that I was doing some work for a few years back. I noticed a white guy intensely going round the stands and picking

---

[5]Simon Rogers, Non-white British population reaches 9.1 million, The Guardian, 19th May 2011.

up information. Talking to him later, he told me that his boyfriend was black and so he wanted information in order to gain a better insight into his partner and the issues that he faces.

I remember going for an event at the theatre in Milton Keynes a few years back and being surprised by the number of mixed race couples. I must confess I was quite surprised when a lady that I know came up to me with two children wanting to introduce me to her grandson. I began to smile at the little white boy, then realised that she was pointing to the little black boy with dreads. Just in case you hadn't realised the lady in question is white. She, however, has a black grandchild because her child is married or living with someone (I'm not sure which) who has a child from another relationship.

This is in effect the reality of the world we live in today and I believe as we go to school and work together and learn more about people from other backgrounds, the more we are likely to mix and form relationships, becoming more mosaic - because whether people like it or not, whether they think it's right or wrong, there is a greater reality and that is we don't choose who we fall in love with.

Accepted Influences or Double Standards

I'm not seeing what you're saying
All the games that you are playing
Look like tactics for delaying
While we're on our knees and praying
Making and breaking
Sitting and debating
The art of speculating
Then accumulating
I'm not buying what you're selling
UB40, So Destructive

There was a point in time, when, in addition to my morning ritual of brushing my teeth, having a shower and putting my make-up on before I left for work, I had to additionally have a nice hot cup of tea. As soon as I got to work, I'd put my bag down, switch on my computer and make myself (together with anyone else around who wanted one) another cup of tea. And so the day would proceed with cups and cups of tea. It's a British thing, isn't it? I mean, good old-fashioned British tea, or rather breakfast tea as we now call it to distinguish between 'proper' tea and the herbal teas, fruit teas, peppermint teas, jasmine and all the other teas that we now drink.

The funny thing is the British probably drink more breakfast tea than anyone else in the world, but to state what is hopefully obvious to most, tea is not actually British, but came to Britain during the days of the British Empire from India and other parts of Asia. Similarly all the sugar that we put in, that we also use to make cakes, biscuits and what have you, came from the Caribbean.

I still believe that the most natural Friday night supper is fish and chips. So do many others. However, there are a lot of people who would much rather have a tikka masala or some other form of curry. They'll even cook it at home. Anyone who has been to India will tell you that the curries that we get from Indian restaurants across the nation are quite different from a curry you would get in India or an Indian home. Curries are, however, Asian rather than British.

In fact, as much as I love my fish and chips, my Sunday roast, sausages and mash, a good steak and kidney pie .... I think it's nice that there are so many other options now available to us such that without travelling too far and I can have an ackee and saltfish pie, sushi, jollof rice or pounded yam, a paella or what have you .... don't you?

It's not just the food, it's music and entertainment as well. Think of how much music has evolved over time and I'm not specifically talking about garage or grime. I think if you go beyond the charts and really listen to music today, you'd be amazed at how varied it is and most of it is a representation of the different cultures that form 21st century Britain. Come August bank holiday this year, as has been the case in years gone and will be in years to come, West London will be buzzing with the Notting Hill Carnival. I think it's fair to say that while the Carnival started as a West Indian event, it has now come to represent the full gamut of British diversity with attendances from all across the world.

Then you come to sports. Let's talk about football for a bit. I think British Premiership football is a true representation of how global the world has become. British Premier League football is truly world acclaimed and I believe that, just as we've got football players from across the globe, the Premiership has also got supporters across the world. In fact, I suspect that there's hardly a country that you would visit where you wouldn't be able to buy a Manchester United, Chelsea or Arsenal t-shirt.

In some ways, the international nature of the British Premiership can be seen as a bit of a disadvantageous to England when it comes to competitions such as the World Cup, as a significant number of our Premiership players end up playing against us for their home countries, but I believe that's just one of those things.

It's not just football though; most sports have players from different backgrounds. Can you imagine British boxing without the excited chanting of "Bruno, Bruno, Bruno" before each of his unsuccessful attempts at a world titles, or the pride that must be gained from watching the unflappable Amir Khan?

Then there are the athletes. We all get behind them and cheer when they are on the tracks competing on our behalf for an event, but what about the thereafter, because there would be quite a significant difference in Britain's medal position at the last Olympics if all our competitors were white and if the competitors of colour weren't British citizens, they wouldn't be able to represent us.

Even the military is not untouched as the one of the highest military awards, the Victoria Cross, was bestowed upon

Grenadian-born Lance Corporal Beharry for valour due to his efforts to save the lives of his colleagues regardless of his own life-threatening injuries whilst serving in Iraq.

To be honest, it's in areas such as this that some of 21st century Britain's greatness can and should be derived from. After all, it is my understanding that a key reason why London won its bid to host the 2012 Olympics is because of its diversity.

A Richer Society: All Just Being

The Concept of Being

I wish I could share all the love that's in my heart
Remove all the bars that keep us apart
I wish you could know what it means to be me
Then you'd see and agree
That every man should be free.
Nina Simone, I wish I Knew How It Would Feel To Be Free

Even if Britain was to close all of its borders today and prevent anyone new from outside from coming in, it would not change the fact that the demographics of the British society have changed and will continue to change on the basis of its current population - most especially in urban areas.

Whilst the overall white British population was still about 5/6th of the overall population as of 2009, with the non-white population continuing to grow, the non-white population is however significantly higher in places such as London, Birmingham, Manchester and Liverpool than certain other parts of the country.

The truth is, even without further migration, the trends are highly unlikely to be reversed. This is especially true when you consider the fact that statistics show that the birth rate of females from ethnic minority backgrounds is significantly higher than white women. I don't see any British government ever (successfully) implementing a China-style one child quota.

It's been said time and time again that you can't choose who you fall in love with. Maybe this is best evidenced in the UK by the increasing number of mixed marriages on the basis of both religion and ethnic origin, such that Britain now has an ever-growing mixed race population. This number is continuing to increase, and unless we want to start to dictate to people who they marry or even just sleep with, then the numbers are going to continue to grow.

Most people who I speak to are happy with the diversity of Britain. The truth is that even Japan, that was previously cited as a country that had maintained its original ethnic makeup, has over more recent years, adopted a much more open policy and become more diverse as it found that its isolationist policies were no longer working.

As we are all destined to live and work together, the question that comes to the forefront of my mind is, "Why can't we all just simply be who we are and be accepted as such?"

It's to this end that I constantly talk about 'Just Being'. You see, life and the people around us can place a lot of expectations on us. I used to feel the pressure of this quite a lot when I was younger, specifically as I didn't seem to fit in naturally anywhere due to my mixed background. However, it got to a point whereby there were days when I decided that I was going to refuse to succumb to the pressures of other people's expectations or even self-imposed pressures, and just be me and do what I felt like doing. I've found that this cannot be done without respect for other human beings.

Furthermore, 'being' may readily work for the individual concerned. However, if we as a wider society are to learn to 'just be' and accept others for who they are, I believe there is a need for a better understanding of identity.

Identity

Babies & children do not see colour,
But the world that they live in does.
Susan Popoola

I have been fascinated by the debates around the adoption of children of black and mixed race backgrounds that have followed the announcement by Rt Hon Michael Gove MP, the Secretary of State for Education, that there was a need to allow responsible white parents to adopt children from such backgrounds. In the debates, many have stated that it is ridiculous to prevent people from adopting a child simply because of skin colour. They've gone on to say that the most important thing is for children to be brought up in a loving environment. They have further gone on to accuse those who have expressed concerns about children of ethnic minority backgrounds being brought up by white families becoming confused and disconnected from their cultural background, as being proponents of something that almost equates to reverse racism.

Personally, I believe that a loving and caring environment is crucial to a child's upbringing and that its provision is not dependent on skin colour. At the same time, I'm also conscious that there is a much bigger, wider world out there beyond the family that a child needs to integrate with and, if parents do not bring a child up in a way to understand this and contend with this from the manner in which people perceive him or her, then the child will ultimately face challenges.

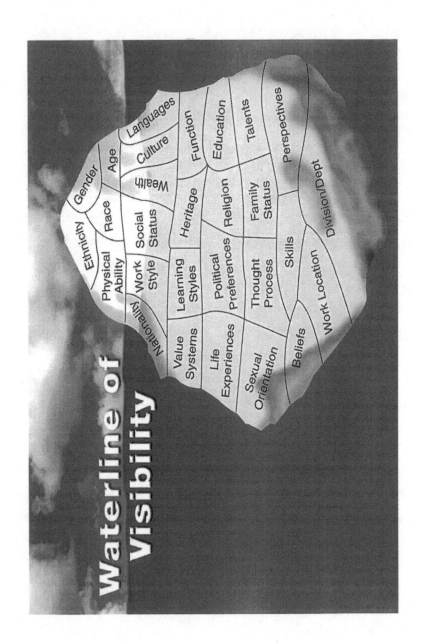

Waterline of Visibility

116

Funnily enough this point was well illustrated by Barak Obama in his book 'Dreams from My Father', when he talks about how he looked through magazines and wondered why he looked different to everyone else and why no one else looked like him. He was brought up by his white family, but went through a period during which he struggled with his identity. It's quite interesting that he identifies himself as African-American and not mixed race.

You see, I believe that this is partly because, regardless of how you identify yourself, there is still a crucial question as to how people identify you. The human tendency is for people to focus on physical attributes and the things that we can see such as gender, age and colour; the things that we can physically see when we meet a person, and, at a secondary level, the things that we pick up from talking to them. There is, however, so much more to our make-up. This is well illustrated by the 'Waterline of Visibility'.

The Waterline of Visibility is based on the concept of an iceberg. The attributes that I have mentioned, that we can see are just the tip of the iceberg, i.e. that which is visible above water. Beyond this there is so much more to our identity which cannot so easily be seen because it is beneath the water surface. This includes our family status, education backgrounds, political preferences, life experiences etc.

These are things that have just as great an impact on identity and who we are as those things that we can see. In order to really and truly understand a person's identity, we need to take the time to look beyond the surface and get to know them.

How Different are We After All?

*While it's easy to focus on our differences of culture and perspective,
let us never forget the values that our people share.
A reverence for family, the believe that, with education, hard work and
with sacrifice, the future is what we make it; and most of all, the
desire to give our children a better life.*
Barak Obama

When you take a closer look at identity, you realise that we are much more complex than just gender, skin colour and, may I add, religion as this, specifically Islam, is so often used to identify and, from a far-right perspective, used as a reason for stating that people should not be accepted as part of mainstream society. While at one level the Waterline of Visibility illustrates our complexities, at another level it highlights those things that we have in common; just as beneath our skins we all have hearts, kidneys, blood running through our veins and all the other essential body parts.

This is possibly better illustrated by Robert Dilts' Levels of Change model (adapted by Maureen Ghirelli).

IDENTITY
I'm a scientist. I'm diabetic.

VALUES & BELIEFS
If only she cared about ... as much as ....
Work comes first. It will take months.

UNCONSCIOUS FILTERS
e.g. MBTI, Metaprogrammes
I prefer the big picture. She leaves things to the last minute.

CAPABILITY
I'm good at thinking on my feet. He doesn't understand how long it takes.

BEHAVIOUR
She said some unpleasant things in that email. He finished that report early.

ENVIRONMENT
I prefer to work in an open-plan environment. They have a fairly relaxed dress code. Physical appearance. Voice.

Dilts' model highlights the things that impact on us and how we behave, which go way beyond identity but extend to our value and beliefs; the unconscious filters that we have that we use to make decisions; our capabilities; behaviour and environment which all come together to make us who we are.

The Need for a Reality Check

Why Can't We Live Together
Sade

My desire to see everyone just freely being is not divorced from the realities of the society that we live in and the challenges of working to understand, accept and embrace each other.

It's a number of years back now, but I can still remember driving in a car with a couple of friends when one turned to me and asked me what was wrong with calling people 'coloured'. She pointed out that someone had told her off for using the word and she hadn't realised that there was anything wrong with it.

I did my best to explain to her the negative connotations from the past of the word, and further went on to point out that my skin colour is natural and not coloured as a picture in a colouring book. I'm not sure that I did a good job, but she's never used the word again. It would be very easy to get frustrated and turn with disdain and say how someone in their thirties could not know that it is inappropriate to call people 'coloured'. The truth is she had previously lived in an area that was all white and so she didn't know better. Whatever the case, I was glad that she felt able to ask me the question, giving me the opportunity to try and explain things to her.

On the other hand, the thing that bothered me was the more recent conversation that I had with her whilst we were out for dinner one evening. As we were generally just eating and talking, a group of people came out from another restaurant and she recognised one of the people who she knew. She wanted to point this out to me and so she tried to describe her to me. She described her height and all of her features, but one. As I realised who she was referring to within the group, I recognised that she had omitted the one unique feature that would have enabled me to immediately know who she was referring to - the colour of her skin - as the lady was the only black person within the group.

This bothers me because it's a minor representation of the political correctness that has beholden our society and holds people like a vice from being themselves and openly expressing themselves. So much so that while I have a degree of understanding for the demise of the golliwog which, though not universal, had a connotation of black people as bad and evil, I cannot understand why children in nursery are no longer allowed to sing 'Baa Baa Black Sheep' unless they additionally sing 'Baa Baa White Sheep'. There are no negative connotations to the song and sheep, black or white, have no relationship to human beings and the colour of their skin.

I believe there is a need for continued dialogue about the issues and areas of society that need to be changed in order for us all to be able to live peaceably in a just society.

American newscaster, Katie Couric, expressed the view that maybe America needs a Muslim version of The Cosby Show because, as she said, "The Cosby Show did so much to change attitudes about African Americans in this country, and I think sometimes people are afraid of things they don't understand".

Some may see this thinking as naive and misguided, but translating this back to Britain, whilst I wouldn't be against it, I wouldn't necessarily advocate a 'Muslim show'; but, come to think of it, there does actually seem to be very little representation of Muslims on television. Now I don't watch EastEnders, Coronation Street, Hollyoaks or the likes so I might be missing something, but I do think it would be useful if these programmes, amongst others, could provide some representation of Muslims on the odd occasion to help provide people with some insight into Islam.

I know there are those who won't like it when I make this comparison, but I do recall hearing about/seeing snippets of EastEnders which had Christian characters. Specially, I saw a documentary on Dot Cotton not so long ago during which there was a discussion about a whole episode of EastEnders which focused on her praying to God and her Christianity, with her being the sole character in the whole episode. To try and pre-empt my critics i.e. those people who don't believe that Islam should be given the same level of importance as Christianity as Britain is traditionally a Christian nation, I will say this is a separate point. I'm not saying that EastEnders or other such programmes should dedicate whole episodes to a Muslim character, but that they could potentially be good vehicles to enable a better understanding of Islam, as other religions.

There is in fact a Canadian sitcom, 'Little Mosque on the Prairie' which has been running since 2007. I can't comment specifically on the impact that it has had, but it must have a degree of popularity to still be running five seasons on, even though it may not give a 100% accurate representation of Islam.

There is, however, a flip side to using television to provide people with an insight into Islam. As I was trying to gain some insight into the impact that 'Little Mosque on the Prairie' has had on the populace, I did a little bit of online research and was actually surprised that a number of Muslims were very critical of the sitcom and how it portrayed Islam.

Furthermore, I am an advocate for a welfare system that helps people through difficult periods in life and supports people who are unable to work for reasons of health or other such reasons. I do, however, believe that there are problems with the system when people opt not to work because they are better off living on benefits. I equally recognise that there are problems with the education system that need to be resolved, so that everyone has a chance of a good education that gives them a fair start in life.

Though I can understand that there are people who may get frustrated by the equality and diversity agenda or, even worse, still call for positive discrimination to favour people who are seen as under-represented, there is a reality that there is still a lot of discrimination within society. The Stephen Lawrence Inquiry that spoke of institutional racism is still not that long ago and the recent 10 year review of the inquiry shows that there is still a lot to be done. There is also a very negative view of Islam.

The bottom line is that there is inequality, there is discrimination - will it ever completely disappear? Maybe not, but I do believe that we must continually work towards a balance, but do so in a way that supports and helps those who are under-represented/ disadvantaged without disadvantaging or over-discriminating against those who are currently not disadvantaged. It's what I refer to as the precious balance in life and this can only be achieved if there is the option for people in all areas of society to openly discuss their concerns, without the fear of being accused in some shape or form, and for others to learn to listen and develop a sense of where people are coming from without concluding that, once something is said that they don't agree with, it means that people are against them.

A Richer Society

We've got to get this world together
Got to keep it moving straight...
If you're rolling to your left
Don't forget I'm on the right
Seal, Get it Together

When I talk about the need for us to all get along, it's not just because of the fact that we are all here to stay, but because there is such richness in our diversity and I sincerely believe that each and every one of us has something unique and special to offer. It's already evidenced in the building of our NHS system with skilled professionals who continually migrate from other countries to support and work alongside people already here. It's in the richness of our music and our food, the way we dress.

There have been numerous debates about multiculturalism and whether or not it has worked. The debate was heightened after a talk that David Cameron gave at a security event when he expressed what were interpreted as negative views on multiculturalism.

I think one of the key concerns is the lack of understanding of a unified definition of what multiculturalism is. The truth is that ultimately there is a need to find a form of multiculturalism that does work as we do, and will always, have differences.

I recently read an article in the Evening Standard that stated that there are now 270 nationalities represented and 300 different languages spoken within London.

Nationality	No of Citizens
Afghanistan	7000
Australia	37000
Bangladesh	37000
Brazil	5000
Canada	14000
China	15000
Congo	5000
France	28000
Germany	25000
Greece	7000
Hong Kong	18000
India	157000
Iran	14000
Iraq	9000
Ireland	42000
Italy	20000
Jamaica	37000
Lithuania	21000
Mauritius	20000
Nepal	13000
Nigeria	68000
Pakistan	35000

Poland	83000
Portugal	26000
Romania	27000
Russia	11000
Sri Lanka	32000
South Africa	52000
Sweden	7000
Turkey	20000
USA	30000
Spain	20000
Zambia	2000

These are official figures from the Office for National Statistics. The thinking is that the actual figures are much higher.

I can imagine if all of these different people are isolated in different corners, speaking their own languages and only interacting with other people when they absolutely have to, then this would create a very negative relationship between neighbours. If, however, people can come together and learn the best of each other's cultures and ways of life, then I believe it will help us to be a much richer, mosaic society.

But it's not just about the culture of different people. All of these people, inclusive of the English, both as peoples and individuals, have unique skills and abilities to offer, which it is foolhardy not to make the optimal use of within society.

I believe true multiculturalism really comes to play when people respectfully interact with each other as who they are - learning not just about the food that they eat, but about those peculiar practices and customs that we all have - most especially those that irk us. The greatest frustration that I have is that these days we criticise multiculturalism without really taking the time to define what it is that we are actually talking about.

The more liberal minds say that they value and appreciate other people's culture, but a lot of the time, what they appreciate does not extend beyond trying food. Most other things remain illogical and strange.

The sad reality is that the deeper questions that we have become too scary to ask, and yet are the very questions that most need answering.

The War for Talent

Anything that's worth havin'
Sure enough worth fighting for
Quittin's out of the question
When it gets tough, got to fight some more
Cheryl Cole, Fight

You might be aware of the war in Afghanistan or Iraq, and potential wars in places such as Ivory Coast and Libya in 2011, but are you aware that there is actually a global war going on at the moment? Because of the recession and the high unemployment rates that exist at this point in time, it's not immediately apparent, but there is currently a global war for talent which will become very apparent by the time we truly get to the end of the recession.

But even now if you look closely and talk to a number of different businesses you will see the signs of it. You will constantly hear employers talking about the need for young people coming into the workplace to have employability skills. Whilst the British NHS is still highly run/supported by a significant number of doctors and nurses originating from Africa and Asia, at the same time there are an increasing number of nurses working within the NHS who are, or are thinking of, migrating to places such as Canada and Australia, due to the better pay and working conditions offered in such countries.

Furthermore, I recently had a conversation with the Managing Director of a small but very successful technology firm. During the conversation, he told me about how his career transitions had brought him to the place of setting up the company. Inadvertently we also spoke about the challenges that he was facing in getting people with the skills that he needed for his business. He further explained that he had got where he was because people had seen the potential in him and offered him opportunities that he hadn't always had the ready skills for, but had supported his development in order to effectively fulfil the role in question. Taking account of this, he pointed out that he was more than willing to cross-train individuals, but had been struggling to fill two particular roles for over six months, even though he had done direct searches, tried recruitment agencies and even the job centre.

This led me to contact a Government Minister, point out my observations and go on to suggest the following.

Considering the current high levels of unemployment that do not discriminate on the basis of qualifications at this point in time, I believe this situation is quite ironic. This led me to think of what solution I would like to see in place to prevent this from becoming a long-term problem for the future.

I would like to see a government skills database in place that highlights skills requirements at a local, regional and national basis, the idea being that employers would enter their key skill requirements into the database. This would provide government at all levels with an indication of the skills requirements at each geographical level and provide crucial intelligence on both current and future needs. The data would feed into educational establishments at both the secondary and tertiary levels, and would feed into decisions about courses to be offered. It would also feed into job centres, outplacement organisations and other organisations working to get people back into employment so as to enable them to work with individuals to develop the required skills.

It is possible that something like this already exists, however, if it does then there are critical questions as to whether it is being used effectively and why the Director that I spoke to was unaware of it.

My dialogue with the Minister is ongoing, but it leads me further to what I see as a blanket argument that currently exists about immigration which does not take a real account of both business and economic needs, together with future implications.

As it stands, we've lost a lot of manufacturing jobs to overseas countries. Currently we have the HSBC talking about relocating to Hong Kong. Further to this, we have recently adopted an immigration policy that will make it increasingly difficult for multinationals to send expatriate managers from other countries to the UK to set up, run or work within offices within the UK. There is a risk with this that such organisations may choose to limit their operations within the UK.

At the same time there are policies being proposed/put in place to minimise the number of foreign students that come to study within the UK. I find this somewhat ironic for two reasons. In the first instance, we recently had the student demonstrations over university fees which have been described as a necessity due to the deficit in university funding. I recently had a conversation with a South African lady currently in a sixth form who had come to England with her parents. We got into a conversation about university and she told me that for the course that she really wanted to study, at her university of choice, she had been told that it would cost her up to £50,000 per annum. I would venture to say that a local student wouldn't pay up to a fifth of this, even with the changes to university fees. Even if you see this as an extreme case, there is still a marked gap between the fees that local and foreign students pay and we are therefore losing out on crucial funding with a knock-on impact on local students caused by the narrowness of our thinking on immigration.

It's possible that some may argue that the advantage gained from overseas students fees may be lost by such students staying within Britain for a period to work. I, on the other hand, would argue that there is something positive in helping to develop individuals who then use their essential skills to contribute to the UK economy before returning to their home country. This is specifically true as foreign students are more likely to study courses in core subject areas whereby they come out with qualifications critical to the economy. It also helps to develop and retain a deep connection between Britain and the students' home countries.

And before you say it, yes there is a high graduate unemployment rate of 20% at this point in time, but I believe most employers would go for the UK graduate if he or she had the same to offer as the foreign graduate.

My thinking on this was further reinforced when I watched a report on how a number of people who studied in American universities were forced to immediately return to their home countries as soon as they finished their degrees due to similar immigration restrictions which sometime force overseas students to return to their home country as soon as they have complicated their qualification. This was great for their home countries, because those highlighted went home to set up very successful companies and jobs at home. The point of the report was that the US lost out, as those jobs could have been created within the US.

I guess the counter argument to this would be that their home countries have an equal, if not greater, need for jobs. My point of view would be - what if such people were able to set up a company in the US, or the UK as the case may also be, and then go on to set up offices within their home country, such that everybody wins and obtains the optimal outcome?

Social Capital in the Workplace

It takes every kinda people
To make what life's about
Every kinda people
To make the world go round
Every kinda people, Robert Palmer

On the soft side of things, talent management within the workplace is important because diverse, mutually respectful, happy teams with shared values perform best. ref: Carol Long, Three Triangles Performance Ltd. This is beneficial for organisations at an individual level, but there is also an economic imperative for effective talent management. I recently read that Brazil now claims to be the fifth largest economy in the world. France is also a threat to Britain's position. This means that Britain is now moving backwards and is potential 'just' the seventh largest economy in the world. Even if Britain has still managed to maintain its position at the moment, where will Britain be positioned in 10 years time if we do not become more strategic in our actions and approach to the management and utilisation of talent?

I believe that we are still in a privileged position where people look up to us and want to work with us or do business with us. There is therefore a need for businesses to create and implement strategies that ensure the effective and efficient development and engagement of the local and global talent offered by all within communities.

At a basic level, there is a need for a clear, strategic understanding of where British industry plans to go within the next 5, 10 and even 20 years. Individual businesses, both large and small, need to have an understanding of where they fit within that plan and what their subsequent strategy to deliver and achieve results is. When we talk about strategy, more often than not, we tend to focus on the operational and financial elements of the business, but we tend to play little attention to the people side of things until there is a more immediate need.

I think the shape of the economy and global talent market that is developing means that this must now change and we must start thinking about people management - or, to be more specific, skills - from a more strategic perspective.

I always advocate for a skills or competency framework approach, which highlights both the immediate and future resource requirements of an organisation from a skills basis.

It means that industry can broadcast skills requirements, such that the education system is best positioned to prepare individuals with the flexibility to meet actual and potential needs and professions that currently don't exist, but which may exist in the not too distant future. It also enables government to have a more strategic, pragmatic view on immigration so that it is aligned to the country's needs, rather than simply pandering to those who are simply and plainly against immigration with a big full stop. It also enables better planning for jobs that may be best outsourced, with the enablement of processes to prepare and redeploy individuals who will otherwise be rendered redundant by such structural changes.

I believe a skills/competency framework also better enables open engagement with the wider community. Where it is clear to people what the competency requirements to work at different levels within an organisation are, it is more difficult for them to claim that they did not get a job because they were discriminated against for one reason or the other. It also better enables people from within the different British communities to mentor and support people from within their own communities to enable them to develop the skills required to obtain jobs at different levels. In fact, I was impressed to go into a McDonald's restaurant recently and pick up a little booklet with the basic framework of the different roles within the organisation and requirements to work at each level.

As we are now what is popularly described as a 'global village', I believe Britain, with its vast diversity, has an advantage as it should be able to use that diversity to effectively interact with and understand different cultures around the world. I believe that British organisations should be mindful of this and look to use this to their advantage.

This, however, will only work if workers also do their part. I believe there are currently too many organisations, especially in retail, where the workforce is highly multicultural but highly segregated. I specifically remember doing some work in one such organisation. I went to their canteen at lunchtime and found that a large proportion of employees sat together with people from the same background as themselves, often speaking in their own language. As highlighted with a recent case involving McDonald's, you can't legislate against this, but I don't believe it is very constructive, and would venture to say that it is a poor reflection of multiculturalism where the gains are minimal.

What About Them Youth?

The streets are supposed to be about different people
coming together
Bringing something new to the floor.
It's not about what you've got, it's what you make of what you've got.
Step Up 2: The Streets

I'm concerned about the young people in our society - not because I believe that they are the terrible, horrible, self-centred people that they are so often portrayed to be. I actually think that they are great, fantastic, phenomenal people with tremendous amounts of character and things to offer, if we just take the time to communicate with them, understand who they are and what they have to offer. As I've found from my interactions with my work as a School Governor, Business Education Partnerships, school talks and former role as a youth worker, I know that there is so much that we can learn from them at so many different levels.

I also believe that for most of them, all they have ever known is a multicultural, diverse (in some, many ways) society; they themselves and their experiences of life are so much more diverse than older generations and that diversity is set to increase as, as already mentioned, increases in population growth will increasingly come from minority groups - even if there was a complete block of migration into the UK from outside of the European Union. The good thing with this is that in so many ways they give me hope as they tend to have fewer prejudices than older people. This was possibly highlighted to me by a recent event.

Someone I know owns a hairdressing salon in Milton Keynes. They do Caucasian hair. I was joking around with her one day, and almost as a dare, I said I would go to the salon one day and ask them to do my hair - just for the fun of it. She gave me the go ahead and so one day when I was at the shopping complex where the salon is based, I walked into the salon with my best attempt at a straight face.

There was a young woman in the salon washing a lady's hair at a sink. She looked up and smiled when I walked in and said hello. I smiled back, said hello and then proceeded to tell her that I would like to have my hair done. She looked at me and very politely explained to me that they were unable to do my hair. Struggling not to laugh, I looked at her with a perplexed look on my face and explained to her that I wanted my hair blonde, just like hers. She explained to me that they weren't trained to do my hair - she suggested other places that I could go to that would be able to help me. I told her that they were too far away and that her salon was the most local to me. I continued to stand there and she pointed out to me that she would speak to the other girls to see if there is any way in which they could be of help to me.

Finally, I left - having a good laugh as soon as I was out of sight. I was impressed. She was only about 20, but her composure was excellent. Not once did she say anything rude or that could be deemed inappropriate that would enable me to turn to her and ask her the question, "Is it because I is black?"

To be honest, I believe young people are naturally less inclined to do so unless they are being out rightly malicious and rude, because they have grown up with people from different backgrounds and are more aware. I believe this is a good starting point for the whole diversity agenda and a reason to hold some optimism.

Admittedly, it doesn't deal with the institutional issues or the inbuilt inequalities, but if people can begin to see more of the interactions and more readily interact with each other, I think we have a good starting point - don't you?

However, I'm further reminded of a recent conversation I had with a friend about Superman. He was bemoaning the fact that it didn't make sense that people didn't realise that Clark Kent was Superman, when the only difference between the two was the glasses that Clark wore. I thought about this for a short while then responded that I actually believed it was very believable as people's perceptions were enough to make them believe that someone wearing glasses could never be a superhero. My friend responded to this - that's true, perceptions can often hide the truth indeed. I guess that's why only the kid worked out who Superman was - the untainted mind. Maybe the rest of us can all begin to renew our minds.

I guess that may lead you to wonder why I started off by saying that I'm concerned possibly not so much about, but more for, the young people in our society - after all, they do seem more inclined to get things right. You see, the problem I see is with the current unemployment rates, are we going to become more creative and give them a fair chance? If not, rather than have them support us in our old age, we are going to be struggling to support them in our old age.

Beyond this, are we going to make them become embittered about their plight in a manner that causes them to begin to, amongst other things, turn on each other and hold each other responsible for their plights?

This would be specifically sad, because in many ways the young people of today are of the most ethical and caring group of people within our societies.

To Conclude

Oh bring back the colour scheme and make me right
Let's start tonight.
Nicki Rogers, Colour Scheme

I spent the Easter of 2011 in a little coastal town named Kingswear, which is just across the river from Dartmouth in Devon.

As a child, my pocket money was almost always guaranteed to go on sweets - these days I hardly eat them. However, as I was embarking on a four hour journey from Milton Keynes to Dartmouth, I decided to buy a small packet of Dolly Mixtures from Tesco to accompany me on my journey. I felt as if I was just eating sugar and wondered why I hadn't just bought sugar. While in Dartmouth, I came across a traditional sweet shop, and both ABC Letters and Dolly Mixtures called out to me. I would like to be able to say that the traditional Dolly Mixtures tasted better than the supermarket ones. In my mind, they did - they had to, or something of my memory of the way things were would just be an illusion. In reality, however, I'm not sure that they really did taste much different. Furthermore, even though I bought them from a tourist area, they were undoubtedly much more expensive than the supermarket version.

But back to Devon; as I walked the quaint little narrow streets, it seemed that on occasion people seemed to look at me a little longer than necessary. It could be because of that spot on my nose (you know, the one that everyone has) that doesn't really exist. It could have been because I was a single female or it could be because - let's face it - I stood out as different because of the colour of my skin. Oh and, of course, it could have been my imagination - a projection of my expectations. Regardless, I exchanged greetings with some people and with others we didn't even look at each other, but all cases we all went our merry ways. I was no trouble, neither were they - they just wanted to get on with their lives.

As I walked - fascinated by the narrowness of the roads and their steepness that led me to constantly pause by the waterside as if to take in the view, but really to get my breath back - I eventually came across a cabin, which was being used as a visitor centre. With the enthusiasm of an explorer, I marched inside wondering what I would discover. I entered to what, I must be honest, was a somewhat bare room with old photographs on the wall and a little black and white telly which documented the history of the area with the instrumental to the song 'Memory' gently playing in the background.

It made me think that, as with most things in life, we can choose to hold on to a romanticised view of Britain that doesn't really reflect the reality of what was, and wish for it back - even though I will bet my life that it will never come to pass. This is not because I don't want it to, but because it's for history and we have moved too far forward; we have all changed too much, as has the world around us, such that it would be no more practical than it would be for an adult to re-live their teenage years.

As the past is not a reality for the future, I believe we need to find a way of moving forward from where we are; appreciating and preserving that from the past and where we currently are that is of importance; embracing new people, things and ideas that can enhance who we are. We must acknowledge and learn from the mistakes of the past without allowing them to cripple us. But, most critical of all, we must do it in a way that respects and, as much as possible, embraces both the value and values of all - inclusive of long-term and more recent residents and even guests for the duration that they live amongst us. As, just as every child within a family is unique with something special to offer, whether he or she is highly academic, creative or what have you, so does every individual within this nation. The only thing is that, with some of us, more time and energy than currently expended is required to find out how a person is best placed, and to develop and engage those (at times) latent abilities in order to both make them feel appreciated and valued, and to enable us to benefit from what it is that they potentially bring.

People, especially from the far-right, often say we've lost the 'great' in Britain. To say that England, and Britain as a whole, does not have culture would be a fallacy and unfair. The truth, however, is that it has evolved over time. More so with the arrival of each new wave of immigrants who both add something and inculcates something new into who he or she is. Whilst this always comes with challenges, to view it as negative, as opposed to the largely enriching evolution that it has been, would be equally unfair and narrow-minded. For I believe it is still there but hidden; hidden beneath layers of dusts of negativity and neglect of things that represent the true value of what we have been, are now, and can potentially become.

It's my hope that consequences can help to stimulate the thinking to facilitate the necessary journey down this path.

In Addition - Don't Forget

About the Author

Susan Popoola *BSc. Dip. PGDip. MA. CIPD FRSA*

Susan has established a successful career primarily as a Human Resources Capital Optimisation Specialist. She has worked on numerous private, public and voluntary sectors HR related projects. On the completion of her first degree in Political Science, she took on the operational role of Computer Executive for an Information Technology company, Popcom Ltd, and shortly advanced to become Business Manager. She took on a consultancy role, reviewing the organisation's operations, implementing a new staffing structure and developing a keen interest in the people aspects of business.

She moved on to work with organisations such as The Novas Group, a multinational housing organisation where she took responsibility for the review of the organisation structure, salary scales and the implementation of an HR System to support the organisation's HR Strategy. Susan has also gained considerable experience delivering on projects for organisations such as WorleyParsons, Ptarmigan Media, Royal Festival Hall, De La Rue, Ove Arup, the Department of Health, MHRA, local authorities, government agencies, News International & a number of SME Businesses.

Significantly she worked with Arup to develop an HR Information Strategy to link the HR Strategy to the overall Business Strategy and enhance the reputation of HR within the business. She has been involved with the Public Sector change agenda, specifically with the Department of Health, where she was involved in the development of a new competency framework and performance management system, and its implementation through the use of new technology, while she developed the Talent and Performance Management Strategy for London Fire & Emergency Planning Authority for close to 6000 uniformed officers.

Early on in her career within Human Resources, Susan recognised the potential for technology to propel HR forward as a strategic business partner. As a result, she has done a lot of work to optimise the use of technology across all areas of HR. This has meant that she has been involved in the planning, implementation and optimisation of HRIS systems such as Oracle & Vizual. Such interventions have enabled HR teams to use technology to work more effectively; reducing time spent on administration and working more strategic. It has also enabled HR staff to quickly obtain HR related information required internally to make factually based decisions and to provide relevant information to both Operational Managers and Board members. While focusing on strategic HR, Susan has stayed up to date with operational issues and employment Legislation, and provides organisations with practical advice on the necessary policy and process changes to both conform with legislation and run an effective business.

Susan also has a keen interest in Business Community Engagement and the Education and Development of Young People with a view to greater Youth Engagement. In line with this, she has been a School Governor of a local secondary school where she sits on a number of Committees inclusive of the committee with responsibility for areas inclusive of staffing Standards and Human Resources, which she Chairs. She is involved in Young Enterprise and acts as a Business Ambassador to a local Business Education Enterprise, gives talks in schools and was involved in the involvement in the new development of the Diploma agenda both via the Department for Children Schools and Families (DCSF) and locally.

She also wrote her first book, 'Touching the Heart of Milton Keynes: A Social Perspective', in 2008.

During her career, Susan has achieved Diplomas in Personnel Management & the Art of Systems Thinking; a Post Graduate Diploma in Human Resources with a specialism in organisational consultancy, and a Masters in Human Resources Strategy & Change. She is a member of both the Chartered Institute of Personnel & Development (CIPD). She is also a Common Purpose graduate and a Fellow of the Royal Society of Arts. Susan's experience in Human Resources has been enriched by the vast amount of experience she has gained working in Operational Management, Career Outplacement, Education Appeals Systems, Systems Implementation & Development, Business Analysis & Investor Relations. Significantly she worked in an Investor Relations capacity on the successful demerger of National Power to form International Power & Innology Plc (Npower).

Susan is currently based in Milton Keynes.

References

Desai, M. (2007) Rethinking Islamism: The Ideology of the New Terror. I.B. Tauris

Equality & Human Rights Commission (2011), Triennial Review 2010: How Fair is Britain? Equality, Human Rights and Good Relations in 2010, The First Triennial Review.

Kirsten Rawlins. MK News (2011) Approval is Given for Mosque in Pub, 20th April 2011, pg 7.

Parekh, B. (2006) Rethinking Multiculturalism. Cultural Diversity and Political Theory, Second Edition, Palgrave Macmillan.

Phillips, M. & Phillips, T. (1999) Windrush. The Irresistible Rise of Multi-Racial Britain, HarperCollins Publishers.

Rollock, N. (2009) The Stephen Lawrence Inquiry. 10 years On: A Critical Review of the Literature, A Runnymede Trust Report.

Sales, R. Editor. (2007) Understanding Immigration and Refugee Policy:. Contradictions and Continuities, Social Policy Press.

Spencer, I.R.G. (1997) British Immigration Policy Since 1939: The Making of Multi-Racial Britain, Routledge.

Visram, R. (2002) Asians in Britain - 400 Years of History, Pluto Press.

Asthana, A. (2010) Why Did Multiculturalism become a Dirty Word? It made Me Who I am, 19 December 2010, The Observer.

Buck, N. Ed (1992) Changing Households: The BHPS 1990 to 1992, The Economic and Social Research Council.

Clay, C., Madden, M. & Potts, L. Eds. (2007) Towards Understanding Community: People and Places, Palgrave Macmillan.

Coultard, M., Walker, A. & Morgan, A. (2002) People's Perceptions of Their Neighbourhood and Community Involvement: Results from the Social Capital Module of the General Household Survey 2000, The Office for National Statistics, The Stationery Office.

Dodd, P. (1995) The Battle Over Britain, Demos

Julios, C. (2008) Contemporary British Identity: English Language, Migrants and Public Disclosure, Ethinic Minority Foundation, Ashgate.

Duncan Campbell. Have You Seen Our Son. The Guardian. Thursday 9th March 2006

Hall, C.. (2001) British Cultural Identities and the Legacy of the Empire, in Morley, D. & Robins, K. Eds., (2001) British Cultural Studies: Geography, Nationality and Identity, Oxford University Press, pp27-39.

Morley, D. & Robins, K. (2001) British Cultural Studies: Geography, Nationality and Identity, Oxford University Press.

Mason, D. (2000) Race and Ethnicity in Modern Britain, Second Edition, Oxford University Press

Darian-Smith, K., Grimshaw, P. & Macintyre, S. (2007) Britishness Abroad: Transational Movements and Imperial Cultures, Melbourne University Press.

Sykes, A. (2005) The Radical Right in Britain, Palgrave Macmillian. Reeves, F. & Seward, E. (2006) From BUF to BNP: Chronology of Racist Extremism and of Opposition to It, Race Equality Practioner Series.

Lloyd, C. NatCen (2009) 2007-08 Citizenship Survey, Identity and Values Topic Report, Department for Communities and Local Government.

Hope Not Hate Leaflet Action. hopenothate.org.uk. Retrieved 2009-10-0

Kelley, L. Ross (2011) The Sun Never Set on the British Empire, "Dominion over palm and pine" http://www.friesian.com/british.htm

Simon Rogers, Non-white British population reaches 9.1 million, The Guardian, 19th May 2011